Cancer, Covid, and Chaos!

JENELLE NOORDAM

CANCER, COVID, AND CHAOS!

JENELLE NOORDAM

Copyright 2022 by Jenelle Noordam
Contact: email - jenellenoordam@yahoo.ca

Layout and design: Heartbeat Productions Inc.(Heartbeat1.com)

All rights reserved. Neither this publication nor any part of this publication may be reproduced or transmitted in any form or by any means, electronic or mechanical, including photocopying, recording or any information storage and retrieval system, other than use of brief statements quoted in reviews, articles, or books without permission in writing from the author.

Printed in Canada

"For I know the plans I have for you," declares the Lord, "plans to prosper you and not to harm you, plans to give you a hope and a future."

Jeremiah 29:11

ACKNOWLEDGEMENTS

To my husband, Dave Noordam - thank you for always taking the time to care for me and for our children. We love you so much and are so thankful for many more years with you!

To my family, my church family, and my friends who have become like family to me. Thank you for every one of you who played a part in my story. No matter how little, I cherish every moment!

To the staff at **Best for Babies** who carried me through two children, covid, and cancer. I love you guys so much!

To Kim for taking so much time out of your days to edit my book for me. I appreciate it more than you know, thank you so much!

Most importantly, to my loving God for ultimately carrying me through chaos. I know He is always right there beside me, walking me through the trials, teaching me lessons I wouldn't normally learn otherwise. Thank you, Lord, for walking with me through the fire and never letting me go.

TABLE OF CONTENTS

Introduction 7
1. January 2020   Beginning of Woes 9
2. February 2020   The "C" Word 15
3. March 2020   Pandemic 25
4. April 2020   Isolation 29
5. May 2020   Coffee Time 33
6. June 2020   Welcome Jeremiah 35
7. July 2020   The Return 39
8. August 2020   Surgery 41
9. September 2020   Happy 40th 45
10. October 2020   Treatment 51
11. November 2020   Breaking 57
12. December 2020   A Lonely Christmas 69
13. January 2021   A New Year 95
14. February 2021   Bittersweet 101
15. March 2021   Moving On 107
16. April 2021   Reminiscing 111
17. May 2021   Speechless 115
18. June 2021   Father's Day 119
19. July 2021   Preparing for Goodbye 123
20. August 2021   Mourning 125
21. September 2021   Taking off Riding 147
22. October 2021   Trauma-versary 155
23. November 2021   Natural Disasters 167
24. December 2021   Change and a New Year 175
25. Talking about Building Connections 183
26. Talking about Mental Health 187
27. Talking about Cancer 191
28. Talking about ALS 195
29. Talking about Faith 197
30. Talking about Writing a Book 201

ABOUT THE AUTHOR

Jenelle, the wife of a cancer survivor, is also a survivor herself. She is a survivor of abuse, a survivor of parental abandonment, and a survivor of mental health struggles. From a young age, she had to learn to face life in front of her and overcome its challenges. Again and again, the devil came against her, sticking obstacle after obstacle in her way. Yet, Jenelle persevered each time, drawing her strength from the God of the heavens. Today she stands tall above the chaos life has handed her way and is proud to share her story with you.

Jenelle Noordam

INTRODUCTION

Christmas 2019 - Life was finally great. After fertility struggles, I not only had a 2-year-old son, but I was pregnant again. My husband was on the mend from his job-induced PTSD. He was getting retrained in a profession less stressful and one he'd be brilliant in. Financially, things were coming together as I had a job I loved, using my class 4 driver's license five days a week. Even my mental health struggles were under control. I have bipolar disorder with a multitude of struggles including a history of suicide attempts. It took years of therapy to help me be the healthiest version of myself, but I did it. Yes, life was bright and clear and hopeful.

CHAPTER 1
JANUARY 2020
BEGINNING OF WOES

So started the beginning of another year. Christmas was over, the holidays had wrapped up, and it was time to resume our regular daily lives. Mine was working a split shift at a daycare driving kids to school and back in a 15-passenger van. I loved it! My two-year-old son, Jesse, attended the daycare during the day. Because we lived a half-hour from my work, I couldn't justify the gas to make two trips each day, so I waited in my van most days in between my shifts. Normally I would take advantage of extra time and maybe get a walk in but let's face it, January is cold! I was also just out of my first trimester of pregnancy, so I didn't have the most energy for walking even on a nice day. I would have loved to sit in some tiny coffee shops but $6.00 a coffee that I can drink in 15 minutes gets too expensive. I only worked part-time and my husband was still on Worker's Compensation Benefits (WCB) from a 2017 PTSD diagnosis. Things were too tight to be buying expensive coffees or driving back and forth to Abbotsford twice daily. A coffee from Tim Hortons and some good reading material was enough to get me through the day.

My job was to pre-trip the bus and make sure it was safe

in every way. When that was done, I drove the school-aged kids to their various schools and then returned the van back to the centre. After I was done picking up the school-aged kids and returning them to the centre in the afternoon, my shift continued working with infants until the centre closed at 5:30 pm. Finally, then, Jesse and I would get in the van and make the half-hour drive home.

We often got home just after 6 pm... and we got home to an empty house. Normally, my husband Dave, would be home but during this time he was studying for new, rewarding work in the human resources field. He took evening classes five days a week. That meant after a long twelve-hour day, I had to drag my cranky two-year old in the house, make him dinner, give him a bath, brush his teeth, and get him into bed by myself... every.single.night. Often Dave would come home from school to see me passed out in the rocking chair in Jesse's room because I just couldn't stay awake. He would wake me up, I would unpack and repack the lunches for Jesse and myself for morning and go right to bed. Five o'clock would come early. I needed as much sleep as I could to get me through this time.

If that weren't enough, it was January. January! The worst month of the year. Not only is the joy of Christmas fading, but I additionally experienced some major life trauma ten years earlier. I am also diagnosed bipolar and have been struggling with my mental health for as long as I can remember. Over the years, as I have struggled, I have learned to be incredibly self-aware. This January I was very aware... aware I was not doing well. My panic attacks had returned, forcing me into this place of not being able to manage. I started experiencing significant cramping which caused me to worry even more about the baby.

I made an urgent appointment to see my baby doctor about the cramping. All he told me was the baby wasn't happy. I didn't even know what that meant. I wasn't happy obviously, but what did that have to do with the baby? He just said the baby wasn't happy. Because of this, he took me off work for the remainder of my pregnancy. With baby's health secured, I could now deal with my own mental health.

I knew what to do. I called my family doctor and got an appointment but that was unfortunately still two weeks away. I called my psychiatrist who was able to prescribe and fax over a pregnancy-safe medication to start.

I reached out to a pastor for advice. Consequently, being off work gave me the chance to journal and process how I was feeling and what was really happening in my mind. Over the next two weeks, I was gradually able to come to a place where I could logically and emotionally handle the life that was about to unravel this year.

Throughout January, my husband Dave had been complaining of a canker sore. In fact, he had been complaining about it for longer than that, but he didn't feel the need to get it checked out. It had been a rough winter and some extra candy eating may have been involved. Either way, the complaining very quickly turned into agonizing pain. If Jesse accidentally hit his cheek while playing, he would double over in pain. Something wasn't right here. Either Dave was being extremely over-dramatic, or something was very wrong.

I happened to have a doctor's appointment booked with our family doctor on January 28th for my mental health. Seeing as I had touched base with my psychiatrist and got on a medication, I gave my appointment to Dave. I told him it's time for him to see a doctor. He thought it was just an ugly canker sore. I thought for sure it was an infection of some kind that was going to require antibiotics. Either way, it needed to be checked. On the morning of the 28th, Dave got ready for the doctor's appointment like it was a regular check-up. Neither of us really thought much about an infected canker sore. The doctor, however, upon seeing the site, felt very differently.

After looking at the infection in Dave's mouth, our family doctor told Dave he was sending him for a biopsy as soon as possible. Dave figured that would probably be a few months due to the wait lists of ENTs (Ear, Nose, and Throat doctors) at the time. Dave already had an appointment scheduled with an ENT for some time in March for a different unrelated issue and, he mentioned this to his doctor. The doctor looked back at him and responded, "This can't wait. I'm concerned this could be cancer."

Dave came home and told me about what the doctor mentioned. I couldn't believe I was hearing the word cancer. It could be false, but something about hearing the word cancer sure sends a vibration straight to your bones. A couple hours after Dave got home from the doctor's appointment, he got a call from an ENT office with an appointment time for the next day. That was very fast! At that moment, we both knew this could potentially be far more serious than we imagined. We had a baby on the way, and I was already struggling with my mental health.

We just couldn't deal with this now. But what choice was there? I was thankful I was already off work. Whatever was about to unfold, we were in it together. I was probably the most scared I had been in my life thus far. I have faced some traumatic, devastating situations but to have my husband be diagnosed with cancer while I'm pregnant with our second child and struggling with my mental health? That's just too much for me.

The next day, Dave went to the ENT appointment and had a biopsy done. When he came home, I could see in his eyes something was different. He was scared. We wouldn't know the results for 7-10 days, but the ENT agreed with the doctor; it looked like cancer.

I couldn't believe this. "God, please don't let this be. I cannot handle that right now" is all I could think. I don't think there was a lot of sleep happening over the next week. We both went to very dark places imaging what this road could possibly lead to. We tried to remain in the moment and in the present but faced with the possibility of a cancer diagnosis, our minds both went to the worst place. We had a two-year-old son and a child on the way. What was this going to mean for our little family?

CHAPTER 2
FEBRUARY 2020
THE "C" WORD

As we turned into February, the tension was tight. We prayed and prayed for good news to come but honestly neither of us could stop thinking about it. Once you hear the word cancer, everything stops and all the "what if's" start to arise. What if it's cancer? What if he needs chemo? What if this is going to kill him? What if he doesn't get to watch his kids grow up? Will he even meet his second-born child? It led us both to terribly dark places despite our best efforts, but it was something with which we just had to trust God. There was nothing more we could do in the moments of waiting but trust; trust that somehow this was all part of God's plan for us.

We didn't know exactly when we would find out Dave's results. The ENT who Dave saw on the 29th had said 7-10 days so each day was an anxious waiting game. On the morning of February 6th, Jesse and I were getting ready to go meet my friend Amanda and her daughter at the trampoline park in Abbotsford. We were about to get our shoes on when Dave's phone rang just before 8 o'clock. We both looked at each other. It was the ENT office.

Our hearts both stopped. We knew. Dave spent about 10 minutes on the phone with the ENT and all I heard come from Dave was "Okay. Yeah. Okay. Yup. Okay. Okay. Thanks."

I brought Jesse into our bedroom to keep him quiet while Dave was on the phone. As he hung up, I could hear him walking toward the bedroom door. Somehow, I knew exactly what he was going to tell me. He looked at me with a glimpse of a tear in his eye. I just asked, "Is it?" and he nodded his head yes while he let the tears run down his cheeks.

As soon as Dave told me it was cancer, I told him right away I would cancel my plans and be home with him. Dave insisted getting out would be good for me, Jesse, and him. He wanted some time to process, and we didn't want Jesse to see too much until we knew what we were dealing with and discussed what and how we would tell him. Plus, Dave now had some bloodwork to take care of and he had to wait around for some phone calls. He was told the cancerous tumour needed to be cut out and he was being referred to a surgeon in Coquitlam.

Despite my best efforts to try and hold it together, I just couldn't. Jesse didn't talk a whole lot then, as he had a mild speech delay, but all he kept saying from the back seat was, "mommy sad." It broke me. He had no idea what was happening or what was potentially going to happen this year. What would I even tell him? What do you even tell a two-year-old who doesn't have the best communication skills?

I felt with the Early Childhood Education I had, and the decade of childcare experience I have done, I should certainly know how to respond to a two-year-old! I honestly didn't know. I just kept driving and somehow choked out, "Yeah honey, Mommy's sad."

As I parked in the parking lot, I could feel my heart beating faster and faster. I parked the van. I could see Amanda had parked beside me. This was going to be tough. I got out of the van, stepped into the rain, and walked over to her vehicle. She rolled down the window, saw the tears in my eyes, and all I had to do was shake my head.

She knew. Dave had cancer. Throughout our twelve years of friendship, we had both faced many things together. This was not something either of us ever envisioned facing, especially in our thirties. The shock was electrifying. This was absolutely life-changing.

Things moved fast. Dave was scheduled to meet the surgeon in Coquitlam that Saturday February 8th, just two days after we got the call that it was cancer, only 11 days since Dave saw the family doctor for his painful canker sore. I knew I had to go in with Dave, but we didn't want to bring Jesse. I didn't want him to carry this emotional weight. We dropped him off with our cousins and headed into Coquitlam.

If it didn't seem real before, it certainly did when we started driving west without Jesse. I didn't go far without Jesse, not unless it was crucial. I hated leaving him. I hated that I had to leave him to go talk about the cancer in his father's cheek. The drive was quiet. Neither of us really knew what to say. We knew we would hold on strong, and we were in this together no matter what was going to happen. We were a team. We were scared, but we were a team in this together.

As we waited in the waiting room, the tension was high. The receptionist came over and called Dave's name. Dave and I walked to the back and entered the little room where we would wait for the surgeon. The wait felt like forever, even though it was only five minutes. Five minutes of waiting and then the surgeon walked in with a chart in his hand.

After looking at Dave, the surgeon explained he would need to cut out the mass. He explained that Dave would be in Vancouver General Hospital for at least one, if not two nights. The hope was that he could cut it out from the inside. If he couldn't, Dave was told he would need to cut it out of his cheek completely, leaving a hole. They would then graft some skin from his arm to cover the spot on his cheek. If that was the case, he would be in the hospital for a week. I couldn't believe all this news I was hearing. It was so surreal.

Two weeks ago, our days were so normal. Aside from me being off work, things were good. Dave was in his last week of classes and was on the hunt for a job while I took some self-care time and prepared to have a baby. Now, suddenly, we were facing cancer, skin grafting, and surgery.

Before we left the office, Dave was given the appointment date for his surgery. It would be at Vancouver General Hospital on February 26th, just 18 days away. What was even more nerve-wracking was the fact the surgeon also had practicing rights at Surrey Memorial Hospital, which was significantly closer to us, but Surrey didn't have an opening until a week after the 26th, and he said this couldn't wait that long.

I had my 20-week ultrasound booked ahead of time, and we were planning on finding out the gender of our baby. We didn't find out with Jesse, but this time I wanted to know.

Unfortunately, the date was booked for February 26th of all days. I called desperately, trying to get an earlier appointment so Dave could know the gender before his surgery but there was nothing available. Everything was unknown currently, and everything was up in the air. I just wanted to know the gender of my baby before all this chaos started. What if something happened to Dave in surgery and he didn't make it out? He had to know if he was having a son or a daughter. A friend of mine graciously offered to cover the fee for us to go to a private clinic just to find out the gender before Dave's surgery. She really wanted us to have something joyful during this time, and it was much appreciated!

    It was finally time to have my ultrasound. Laying there on the bed, I felt the cold jelly being rubbed all over my belly. This was it. We were going to find out what we were having. I felt like it was a boy. I don't know why because this pregnancy was far different than Jesse's, but I just had a feeling. We saw the head followed by the shoulders, arms, stomach, and… I was right. We were having another boy! Obviously, God felt a boy is what we needed at this time, and we trusted Him.

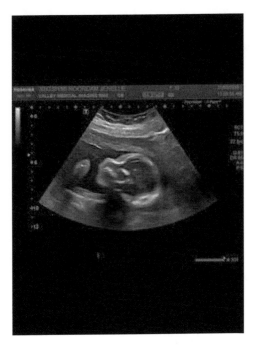

Ultrasound photo of baby boy

The day of Dave's surgery quickly approached with our heads full of tension and anxiety. Dave had to check into the hospital in Vancouver at noon and the procedure was set for 2 pm. We were told it would be a 30–45-minute surgery and then 2-3 hours for recovery before I could see him. As we were waiting for 2 pm to come and as Dave was constantly being questioned and poked by nurses, doctors, and the anesthesiologist, we decided to talk names for our son. So far, we hadn't been able to agree on one. While we were waiting though, Dave told me a few nights ago, when some dear friends were over praying for us, he felt the name Jeremiah come to mind. He really wanted us to have a constant reminder of God's plan for us no matter how bleak the situation looked.

In the Bible, the verse Jeremiah 29:11 says, "For I know the plans I have for you," declares the Lord, "plans to prosper you and not to harm you, plans to give you hope and a future." We knew somehow, some way; this was all part of God's good plan for us. We just didn't yet know how.

After Dave went into surgery, I waited in the waiting area with my in-laws. Modern technology these days allowed us to see which room he was in since they gave him a GPS ID bracelet (Yeah, pretty cool!).

We were told he would be in the operating room for about 45 minutes. It was an anxious 45 minutes. We found his number on the TV screen (they had multiple TVs around which scrolled through pages of patient numbers and locations like an airport arrival/departure screen). By 3 pm, it said he was still in the operating room. I thought it was only 45 minutes. At 3:30 pm, he was still in the operating room… 4 pm still in the operating room. I was afraid my worst fears had come true. I feared for some reason he wasn't going to make it through the surgery. Why else would a 30–45-minute surgery still be going on past 5pm? Finally, we saw his number change locations… he was in recovery. What a rush! I didn't know if we were in the clear, but this was a good sign.

My in-laws decided to go home then since it was getting dark and raining. It was over an hour drive home. I couldn't go. I couldn't leave Dave. I had to know he was alright. I had to talk to him. I called the recovery room, and they said he wasn't there yet but to call this other number. I called the other number, and they didn't know where he was. I was getting so frustrated. I just wanted to know if he was okay. Why couldn't anyone just tell me?

I couldn't handle waiting in the hospital anymore. I wasn't going to leave, but I couldn't stay in the building. I chose to walk back across the street and wait in the van. I listened to music and worried. I tried to pray but my anxiety just got the best of me. I simply felt blocked and numb.

Finally, at 7 pm I got a phone call. I thought it must be the nurses to tell me he's okay. Better, it was Dave himself! I can't explain how instantly my shoulders relaxed, how quickly the weight in my chest eased and I could breathe again. Dave was okay. I asked him why it took so much longer than necessary, and he said it was because they didn't have a bed ready in recovery! Such a simple answer, and yet I spent hours fretting about it. I try not to let my anxiety get me but sometimes I just can't win the battle. I thanked God immediately my husband, my best friend, was okay. He wasn't leaving me.

During times like this, I like to stop and just take a minute to think about all the hours I spent stressing rather than trusting in God's plan. God has a plan, and He promises His plan is for good. Me stressing and worrying did not change that plan, and it did not help me any in that time. It's hard to do in the moment of high stress, but I must remember to pray and talk to God about it. He wrote the Book of Life; He knows how it ends. He is the author of all our stories. He may not fill me in, but He is there to walk me through the story.

After I got off the phone with Dave, I was able to go and see him for a few minutes. He was in recovery, so they typically didn't allow visitors, but they made an exception for us for 5 minutes. In that short 5 minutes, we talked and decided our son would, in fact, be named Jeremiah. We trusted God's plan and it felt like the rightest name in the world. For whatever reason, we felt confident Dave was meant to have this cancer battle. We both felt it. We trusted God's plan going forward, whatever it looked like, and choosing the name for our son was the perfect way to remember God's promise.

After a long day of anxiously waiting, I began the long drive home. It was over an hour in the dark and rain. I don't know what was going through my head, but I was suddenly so overwhelmed. I was also driving through Vancouver, which I was not familiar with. I was crying and crying as I tried to see the road markings between my tears and the rain. The surgery went well. Dave fought a cancer battle. What was the big deal? Why was I being an emotional wreck? I felt like I needed to stop, to think clearly but I missed Jesse so much I couldn't stop. I needed to get home, but I needed help to get there. I called a friend who stayed on the phone with me while I cried my way through Vancouver. I made it to the freeway and breathed a sigh of relief. Now the homestretch. I would soon see my precious little boy whom I missed so much.

When I got home, Jesse was already asleep. Apparently, he cried himself to sleep. Oh, my momma's heart was so broken. As soon as my friend left, I went to his room, scooped him up out of bed, and brought him to bed with me. There was nothing I wanted more than to be close to my son. I missed my husband terribly much, but he was okay now and in good hands. Now it was my turn to relax and take care of my needs. I needed my son so much, and I knew he needed me. He cuddled me instantly. His body melted against mine, and I was so happy for this snuggle. I felt terrible leaving him for that long, but this journey was over now, hopefully.

The next day, Jesse and I got ready to go pick up Dave

from the hospital. I did well on the drive in, considering how much city driving causes me anxiety, and this time I was alone without Dave guiding me where to go. We made it, thankfully, and headed inside. As I walked through the hospital doors, I remembered where to go. I sanitized my hands and went down the hallway, to the left, and into the elevator. When we got to the unit where Dave was, we had to be buzzed in. As soon as we got in, Jesse spotted him before I did and went running to him. He missed his Daddy so much!

Dave shocked me when we were preparing to leave. He had just had surgery on the inside of his mouth to remove a tumour, and he looked at me and said, "Do you want to go for lunch?" I wasn't sure if he would be able to eat or drink anything, let alone "go for lunch." In fact, we had been talking prior to his surgery about liquid diet foods for him to eat after his surgery. But he seemed confident he could, so we made it a plan. We found our way to the Cactus Club and sat down for lunch. Dave wasn't finished there. He also wanted to go have a tour of the SportsNet 650 studio because it was right around the corner. I expected to pick up a groggy post-surgery patient and bring him home. Going for lunch and a studio tour was not what I was expecting.

We wouldn't know any results from the surgery until he could see the surgeon again which would be on March 14th. We would have to go the next two weeks wondering if the surgery was successful. We wanted to trust God, but I can honestly say there were doubts. After all, this was cancer! In the meantime, Dave would have to recover from his surgery, and we would continue with life, hoping for the best news possible in two weeks' time.

CHAPTER 3
MARCH 2020
PANDEMIC

To say March started out with a boom would be the understatement of the year. Our little family was still in between Dave recovering from surgery and anxiously waiting to find out if the surgeon successfully got all the cancer out.

The rest of the world was an anxious wreck for another reason. Slowly throughout the year so far, a virus later known as COVID-19, spread its way throughout the world and into Canada. By March 11th, the WHO declared COVID-19 a pandemic. It was honestly a lot to take in. We weren't done with cancer; we were preparing to have a baby and what? A Pandemic???

Within just a few days, the NBA, NHL, and most other sports leagues suspended their seasons, the JUNO awards were postponed, all nonessential businesses were told to temporarily shut down, and everybody was told to stay home and not go out unless it was essential.

Even schools were not returning after spring break. This was unlike anything we or anyone we knew had ever experienced. Here we were anxiously awaiting if Dave was going to be cancer-free, but we were right in the middle of chaos.

Was Dave's cancer going to be gone? What sort of life would we return to in the middle of a pandemic? And how were we supposed to bring a child into the world in a few short months when no one in the world knew what tomorrow held?

As the date with the surgeon approached, we both felt the anxiety everywhere. The tension was high, sleep was little, appetite gone. Were we going to be lucky enough to be done with this cancer journey? Or was this not yet over?

We walked into the doctor's office and very quickly saw how times had changed. The COVID-19 pandemic was circulating and efforts were being made to stop the spread. Notices were put up informing patients of COVID-19, staff were asking each patient covid-related questions, and if you had any signs or symptoms of covid, you were kindly asked to go home and rebook your appointment. We really were in the middle of a pandemic, and about to find out whether Dave's cancer surgery was a success or if he would need further treatment. The nurse called Dave's name and we walked from the waiting room to the doctor's office where we would sit and wait for the surgeon.

We waited in the quiet, not sure what to say. Finally, the surgeon walked in. He pulled open the file in his hand and showed the paper on top to Dave. He explained to him this paper was his post-surgery results. All the outside layers of the skin cut out were benign. I think I knew what that meant, but I needed further clarification. Dave did too as he asked, "So you got it all? I am cancer free?" to which the surgeon responded, "Yes, I got it all. You are cancer free." Of course, he would still need regular check-ups every 3-6 months for the next few years and there was always a chance it could come back but for now, it was gone!

Wow! What a whirlwind of emotions. The relief that instantly fell from our shoulders was unlike anything I had felt before. I don't think I had ever felt so much relief in my entire lifetime. Dave was cancer-free. I was so happy I could almost not believe it. From the date he saw his family doctor to the date he was considered cancer-free was only six weeks.

How could we have gone through so much emotion in six weeks? I wondered about the state of the baby with all this stress, but I trusted God would not give me more than I could handle. So, it's done. It's really done. We could move on and get back to normal... except what was normal in the middle of a pandemic?

CHAPTER 4
APRIL 2020
ISOLATION

    Initially when COVID-19 started circulating, Canada was asked to shut everything down and stay home for two weeks, then four weeks, then six weeks. At first, it honestly was nice, a little scary, but nice. So far 2020 had started out with my poor mental health and then Dave's cancer. I kind of needed an excuse to not go anywhere and just be home with my family for a while. In fact, we took the opportunity to potty train our then 2 ½ year old son.

    We did what we could to make the best of things at home. We found a giant box and used it as a fort in the middle of the living room. We cut open a door, a couple windows, threw a blanket overtop, and it was the most amazing place to be! Eventually we brought a bunch of markers to colour inside the box. Jesse scribbled miraculously, about as well as a two-year-old can! I wrote the ABC's and numbers 1-20. I wrote our family members names, friends names, colours, shapes, and so many more things. It was great! We even put his mini trampoline in there for him.

Our son Jesse peeking out of the fort

The other thing I did with Jesse was make isolation play dough. Back when I had a daycare, before I had my own kids, I would do all sorts of fun things with them. When I had my own, and by the time he was at the right age, I was back to work. This was now the perfect opportunity to do all those fun Early Childhood Education (ECE) activities I had too much fun learning in school. He chose play dough and I thought I'd get creative with the pandemic and call it isolation play dough. Something different maybe? Jesse got to pull up a chair at the stove. He got to pour all the ingredients into the pot and stir it all together. Then I turned on the back burner and did my part while it was hot. He was so excited to watch and be a part of it.

Jesse and Mommy making isolation play-dough

We got creative through April, finding clever ways to do the things we normally do but in a much different way. One of the things Jesse and his best friend used to enjoy doing together when they visited was playing in the bathtub. They were only two years old and loved to splash and play with water toys together. Now, since we couldn't have in person visits because of the pandemic, we improvised. They did bath time together through video messaging. It wasn't the same obviously, but it was so silly that it got the kids to have fun spending some quality time together.

On the nicer days, we would go out on Jesse's bike and watch him go up and down the street, zooming past us. We got him a balance bike in hopes that he could learn the art of balancing on a bike without pedals before learning how to pedal. The hope was that he would be more easily able to learn how to ride a pedal bike later down the road and then one with no training wheels.

The bizarre thing about being out on Jesse's bike was how quiet the neighbourhood was. The sun was shining, schools were not in, and everybody was inside their house as quiet as could be. All the cars were still parked along the street as if it was the weekend when all the families were home. It was eerie. I couldn't get over the fact we were bringing another child into this. All the worries that ran through my head were constant. It took everything I had to trust, trust the Lord with my life and the life of my family.

As the month of April went on, it felt like we hadn't left March yet. The kids went on spring break, everyone stayed inside, and nothing had changed - except the COVID-19 numbers. They kept rising. Despite the efforts of all the health protocols, it was still circulating too quickly. By the end of April, already 100 people had died of COVID-19 in the province of British Columbia, where we live. The numbers projected at that time, stated that depending on the containment efforts, between 4,000 and 300,000 people in Canada could die from COVID-19 over the course of the pandemic!

CHAPTER 5
MAY 2020
COFFEE TIME

As quickly as March turned into April, April turned to May. It was time to start preparing for our new baby boy arriving in a couple of months. It seemed Dave's cancer really was gone. Despite not being able to open his mouth very far, he felt great! There were no signs of cancer in his mouth or anywhere else. Aside from this pandemic we were still in, I was finally relaxing and thinking about preparing to give birth to my son.

Being pregnant with my second child, I felt I needed to get out more than I was. I couldn't really go visit anyone because of the pandemic restrictions, but my dad lived a 15-minute walk away. I had a talk with him one day about being each other's safe house during this time when we technically weren't allowed to be mingling in other people's houses. I really felt that for my mental health, I needed at least one place where I could go to feel safe. That place was my dad's.

Jesse and I ended up walking down to my dad's house almost every day. If I was equipped with snacks and a tablet, Jesse was happy. I got coffee, company, a break from staring at the same four walls, and it broke up the day. The exercise was good for the little one I was carrying around in my abdomen too!

As the days went on, the restrictions went on too. I was spending more and more time at my dad's house. I even had my own supply of coffee and cream there! Dave was currently home, job searching as he had just come out of school. My dad's place was a good place for Jesse and me to go while Dave spent numerous hours on the computer searching.

After a few weeks, the number of people congregating at Dad's "safe house" increased. There was his fiancé Kim, her daughter Connie, Kim's son-in-law Ed and her three grandkids. This was wonderful for Jesse as he hadn't played with anyone since the pandemic hit. Nobody had. It was awful and terrible for mental development and the needed skills to learn and adapt to life.

By the middle of May, we were having regular coffee visits at Dad's with Connie and her kids too. It was so nice to see Jesse interacting with other kids. Connie's youngest daughter was only a year older than Jesse. They each had skills to teach each other, and it was so cute to watch!

Throughout May, the kids bonded, as did Connie and me. Since my dad and Kim were set to get married, I naturally saw Connie as a stepsister. In fact, my dad and Kim were supposed to get married Victoria Day weekend in May of 2020. They had it all planned out to get married at the campground where all their friends and family get together to camp for the May long weekend. Unfortunately, camping was one of those things taken away by provincial health orders so they decided to postpone it a year. Getting married at the campground was important to them, so they chose to wait until the next year or possibly the year after when the pandemic was over and done with.

CHAPTER 6

JUNE 2020

WELCOME JEREMIAH

As June began, restrictions surrounding the novel coronavirus, COVID-19, were starting to ease. We were able to see a few people again with a few restrictions still in place. We were still not able to attend our church. We were not allowed to have more than six people in our home. We were not allowed to gather in groups of more than 50 people outdoors. That meant weddings, funerals, and other large gatherings for the summer were either cancelled or very limited in their capacity. Restaurants were allowed to open back up but only at 50% capacity and only with proper health protocols in place. Sports games were back on the air, but not in person. The stands remained empty while the players played for the cameras. Doctors, counsellors, and other medical professionals did their appointments online or over the phone unless it was urgent to be seen. It wasn't really "normal," but it was better than anything else this year had brought so far.

Things had been going well but there was one thing looming over our heads. Dave had a check-up with his surgeon coming up. He wasn't having any issues or symptoms, but it's common practice after having cancer to get checked regularly. This was check-up number one. We hoped and prayed with everything already going on with the pandemic and preparing for our baby any day, we were not going to go down this road again, but also trusting in God's plan for us. June 13th came quickly as we prepared for Dave's appointment. Only this time I couldn't go with him. Health protocols surrounding COVID-19 were constantly changing. Doctor's offices such as the surgeon's office, were telling their patients they now had to come alone with no support person with them. This was hard for us. Dave had to go to Coquitlam, sit in a waiting room, sit in an office, and wait all alone. I was at home with Jesse preparing to have our baby any day anxiously waiting to hear if everything was still okay.

Finally, I got a call from Dave. Everything looked great according to the doctor. Thank you, Jesus! He checked Dave all over and said he had no concerns. They scheduled another follow up for three months later, but today the doctor had no worries. It was hard for Dave to go there alone but at least today he went there for good news. Now we could get back to preparing for baby Jeremiah.

Jeremiah was measuring big. An ultrasound at 36 weeks measured him at that time to be approximately 9lbs 4oz! I still had another month until my due date. Given the extremely horrendous labour and delivery of my first-born largely due to his size, I did not want to put myself through that again. I opted for a planned c-section for the morning of June 30th. It felt so nice to feel prepared this time. That date fell one week before my delivery, so it was doubtful, I would go into labour early. It gave us time to prepare our firstborn about what day he was going to become a big brother and how he was going to have a sleepover with his best friend Emma while we go have the baby.

Jeremiah seemed to have a plan of his own for delivery. On the morning of the 29th, I woke up at 6 o'clock with contractions. I tried to ignore it, but they were persistent. I laid in bed timing the contractions until 7 when I woke up Dave to tell him I was in labour. He instantly panicked, "Call the midwife! Call Mom and Dad!"

I, on the other hand was somewhat delusional... I wanted a shower first. For whatever reason, I really needed to shower, and blow dry my hair and straighten it. Dave packed the rest of the bag and got Jesse ready to go see Grandma and Papa while I called the midwife and explained where I was at - clearly in labour.

The drive to the hospital was terrible. We lived 30 minutes away and we had to drive down a long, winding road full of potholes to get to the freeway. We made it, although I couldn't walk very well. We asked for a wheelchair but due to COVID-19 they only had them at the main entrance, and you had to go get it yourself. I seriously wondered about some of these health protocols but now wasn't the time. I had to walk to the elevators and get myself up to the 4th floor to have this baby!

Back in February, we had chosen the name Jeremiah after the Bible verse in Jeremiah 29:11. We fell in love with it and held onto that hope. A few weeks prior to my due date, my friend suggested how funny it would be if Jeremiah was born on the 29th at 11 o'clock. Well now here I am in labour on the 29th at 9am... telling the nurses to time my c-section for 11! I wanted to hold that baby in for another two hours. Obviously, our bodies do as they do in labour and doctors can only move at their speed, so I really had no say. God did though.

Shortly after 11am, Jeremiah William Daniel Noordam was born weighing a whopping 10 lbs 05 oz!

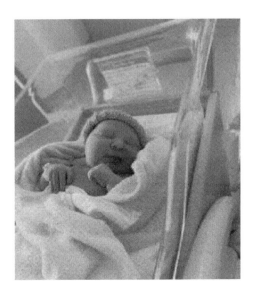

Baby Jeremiah

The next day, we were discharged and able to go home. Bringing Jeremiah home was so exciting. I remember leaving the hospital with Jesse terrified of how I was going to keep this little human alive. With Jeremiah, there was excitement in the air to add him to our family and for the brothers to finally meet.

When Jesse first saw us walk in the door at home, he came running to me. Of course, I had to be careful because of the caesarean but I missed him so much. I wanted to just lift him up and squeeze him so tight, but it would be weeks before I would be able to lift Jesse. In the meantime, gentle hugs would have to do, and we had lots of those.

CHAPTER 7
JULY 2020
THE RETURN

Restrictions were lifted somewhat in July, so we were able to enjoy seeing a couple of friends and getting outside to the park and for some walks. We were settling into the groove with the new baby. Jeremiah was a mellow baby and Jesse did well to adjust to him too. Jesse kept asking when the baby could go play in his room, oh my heart. He had such high expectations that his little buddy was going to come out of the womb ready to run off playing. But first, we would get to watch this little guy grow up and appreciate the very short time he was this small.

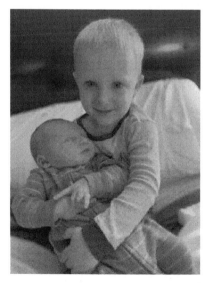

Jesse with baby Jeremiah

I was sure there would be good days and bad days, but for now, we got to enjoy our little family of four with carefree hearts, until Dave looked at me one day and said, "I just wanted you to know I made an appointment with the doctor." Puzzled, I asked him why, but I almost knew without needing to ask. Then he showed me the lump in his neck almost the size of a golf ball. My jaw dropped and my heart sank. I begged God not to do this to us again but at the same time tried my best to trust Him.

As we suspected, the family doctor who saw the lump was concerned. He referred Dave back to the surgeon to get it evaluated and get a biopsy. The appointment with the surgeon was scheduled for July 23rd, and again, Dave had to go alone because of the current restrictions. The surgeon explained that it had to be cut out, so Dave would be needing another surgery. He still had to go for a CT (computed tomography) scan though to determine the approximate size of the tumour in his neck.

By the end of July, we were celebrating our baby turning just one month old while starting our second cancer journey of the year. Over the next couple weeks, Dave had another biopsy, appointments with an anesthesiologist, a covid test, and a scheduled surgery set for August 19th. I really thought this was over. I was hopeful it was anyway. I was very wrong.

CHAPTER 8
AUGUST 2020
SURGERY

Typically, Dave and I start out August in good spirits because our anniversary is in August. Normally we go out to a restaurant and maybe a movie, but because of Dave's upcoming surgery and the current pandemic, things looked a little different this year. For starters, Dave wasn't allowed to go into any public places until after his surgery. The doctors didn't want to risk Dave catching COVID-19 and not be able to have the surgery in time. We picked up some food to go and sat by the river for a picnic. It was nice!

The 19th of August came quicker than expected. It was so much harder than his first surgery. He wasn't allowed to have anyone even come inside the hospital with him. He was to be dropped off out front of the hospital and go in completely alone. He had no one with him by his side to face the removal of yet another tumour. He had no one to wait with, no one to be there waiting for him when he was done. He was alone. He was alone in the hospital while I was single parenting our two boys alone at home. Jeremiah wasn't even two months old yet.

After the surgery was done, Dave Face-Timed me on my phone and boy was I shocked when I saw him. Happy but shocked. The tumour was supposed to be 2cm in size. I was therefore expecting about a 3cm mark stitched up. Instead, he had 25 staples from under his right ear to under his chin on the left side, eight inches from end to end. I don't know what it quite was, but my gut did a flip right then and there. This didn't seem right. Why did they need to cut 8 inches to remove a 2cm tumour? Something didn't seem right. I asked Dave about it, and he had no idea. He was quite impressed with the giant battle wound he got from his surgery, though. He seemed in surprisingly good spirits so I thought I would leave it alone and figure out the answers the next day.

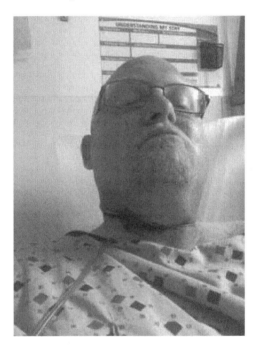

Dave showing off his incision

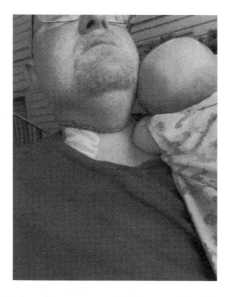

The next day, Dave was discharged and ready to come home. Again, no one could go inside and see him or help him get his stuff ready. He was to get himself down to the door with the help of a staff member, and his ride could pick him up there. It was so crazy how times had changed from his surgery in February to his surgery now. I couldn't believe it. Regardless, I was thankful he was done, home, and safe. Now he had to keep the staples in until the 26th when he would go see the surgeon again for staple removal and an update on why his incision was so large.

As we prepared to go see the surgeon on the 26th, the anxiety was hitting. Last time he got lucky. Would he get lucky enough this time? My friend Jordan came to watch the kids so we could make a "date" out of it and at least drive in together. I still couldn't go into the building with him, so I would have to wait in the car, but he had 25 staples in his neck. He couldn't exactly drive himself there this time anyway. Halfway to the appointment, which was over an hour away, the office called us and regrettably apologized but needed to cancel the appointment. The surgeon was currently caught up in a surgery and would not be available to meet us in time. The receptionist kindly told Dave he could go to his family doctor to have the staples out, and as for the conversation regarding the surgery, the surgeon would call Dave later and arrange for it to be a phone appointment.

As we could no longer go see the doctor but had already decided to make a date out of it, we went for dinner. It was the first time since having Jeremiah that Dave and I were able to get out just the two of us. It wasn't exactly the scenario we were envisioning, but it was nice, nonetheless. We went for dinner together in Langley and then headed home to our boys. About 15 minutes from home, Dave's phone rang, and we saw it was the doctor's office. I pulled over and intensely watched the look on Dave's face change as the doctor spoke to him. I wanted to know what he was saying so bad. I willed myself to be able to hear, but I just couldn't. In the end, Dave hung up the phone, looked at me and told me he needed a minute. My heart sank.

Dave explained to me the surgeon was surprised to find that not only was the tumour significantly larger than the CT originally showed, but it had also ruptured in Dave's neck. Because of this, the surgeon had to go through five levels of the neck and remove 78 nodes which were affected by the ruptured tumour. Because of this rupture, the surgeon explained to Dave he would need further treatment, radiation. We didn't know when this would start or what it would look like yet. We just knew that his file was being sent to the cancer centre in Abbotsford, and he would be followed by a team of doctors there.

CHAPTER 9
SEPTEMBER 2020
HAPPY 40TH

The first appointment with the cancer centre was scheduled already for September 1st, six days after finding out the surgery was not fully effective and Dave would require further treatment. During this appointment, he found out he would need dental surgery done at the BC Cancer Centre in Surrey because certain treatment can be risky after radiation treatment. He also needed to meet with a medical oncologist, an audiologist and have a PET (positron emission tomography) scan before radiation could start. Moreover, restrictions surrounding COVID-19 were once again being tightened as the numbers were going up. Dave was also celebrating his 40th birthday this month. It was certainly a lot. September a year ago was so normal. Now I'm supposed to figure out a 40th birthday during a pandemic with a new baby and cancer on my mind?

Luckily my sister-in-law took over the birthday celebration for Dave. She has a large property full of greenhouses, so she set a 100% covid friendly family birthday party equipped with a full buffet, balloons, separate seating for each family, and of course masks and hand sanitizer. It made for an amazing memory!!

She set up six different picnic tables all facing each other in a giant circle. Dave's parents had one, and each of the five siblings with their spouses and children had a table. We maintained social distance as per COVID-19 protocols while still managing to celebrate this amazing person Dave is. It was nice to have something fun and exciting before all the seriousness of cancer took over.

Dave's birthday family photo

Dave's appointment with the medical oncologist was scheduled for the 22nd. We didn't know beforehand what the point was in meeting with two separate oncologists, but we knew after. During this appointment, the medical oncologist explained to Dave news we were not expecting. Due to the reoccurrence of this cancer already, if the treatment didn't work or if the cancer returns afterward, it would then be considered terminal, and Dave would have one to two years to live. Because of this, the doctor highly recommended Dave do chemotherapy as well as radiation to increase the chance of success. He would have six rounds of chemotherapy and 30 sessions of radiation over the coming weeks. The oncology doctor believed the two together would be about 75% effective.

That was hard news to hear. How could it get to this point? We had an almost three-year-old and an almost three-month-old. Dave can't get a terminal cancer diagnosis. He was only 40. How could life change so fast? I prayed day in and day out for that not to be the case, but the fear was crippling. Here is when it counts to have faith, the faith to know that no matter what happens, it is part of God's plan, and His plan is for good.

Dave's PET scan was scheduled for September 26th. Because of the radiation that is injected for the test, he was not allowed to be around the kids for 6 hours after the test was complete. This meant, once again, I was on my own for the day. Dave went into Vancouver with his dad and then stayed with them at their house for the remainder of the time until he could come home again. We were all excited for the next day, though, where we would be getting Jeremiah dedicated at church. This is a ceremony that dedicates the baby to God and welcomes the baby into the church. During the ceremony, the parents also dedicate themselves to raising the child as a Christian.

For a short time, churches were allowed to have in-person services, but there were many restrictions. There was a 50-person limit, masks were mandatory, seating was spaced throughout the sanctuary for each family, hand sanitizing stations all over, and there was no live music, no childcare, no Sunday school, no coffee, treats, or Sunday hugs. September 27th was the only time we were able to make it to church, and we thought dedicating Jeremiah now would be ideal, especially since the sermon was being live broadcasted online. We didn't know if we would make it back to church at all. It depended on when Dave's cancer treatment would start and what restrictions would be in effect.

In the meantime, Dave was starting work again now of all times. He had been on WCB (Worker's Compensation Board) for his 2017 PTSD diagnosis, but the payments were now stopping due to how long he had been out of school. They obviously didn't take into consideration the cancer dilemma in the middle of a pandemic. Either way, Dave was forced to return to work. He was hired by a local company as a lead inventory coordinator. His job would consist of finding ways to improve inventory accuracy on materials and products. It was probably a good thing for him to work to take his mind off things, at least for now.

One thing I set in place for Jesse for this time was daycare. I felt I was already carrying a heavy load with not knowing what this season was going to look like. I was struggling with meeting all of Jesse's needs, taking the time to process cancer treatment for Dave, and taking care of the baby. Jesse and I talked about daycare and what it would be like for him. He came with me to tour one, and he liked it so much, he wanted to stay there immediately even though the centre was already closed. I knew this would be good for him as we started this season in our lives.

Jesse ready for his first day of daycare

Jesse started daycare at the end of September. The first day was hard. He was so excited to go, but when it was time for me to leave, he cried and cried. I work in childcare, and I am very much aware it is like ripping off a band aid, you just must go. I gave my boy a hug and kiss while the teacher held him, and I walked out the door. It was so tough to see my boy struggle, but I knew this would be for good.

CHAPTER 10
OCTOBER 2020
TREATMENT

As we moved into October, we knew treatment would be starting soon, but we did not know quite when. In the meantime, Dave was back to work. This was a new job, and so far, they had been so understanding of Dave's cancer appointments and missed time from work. We felt so blessed to have this stability of a job for Dave to carry him through this.

Thanksgiving weekend (Canadian Thanksgiving is the first weekend in October) came and went quickly, but because of stricter COVID-19 health protocols, we were not allowed to have anyone come over to our home. We were only allowed to socialize with the people who already lived in our home. Luckily, we lived in the basement suite of my in-laws, so we did get to have some family around for Thanksgiving. It was also Jesse's third birthday that weekend and Dave was starting chemo and radiation the following Tuesday. It was a busy weekend but also the beginning of a season we would surely not forget. We also had just recently found out the PET scan showed the cancer had spread to his left side. The oncologist, therefore was sending Dave for seven weeks of treatment, not just six.

Dave's treatment started on Tuesday, October 13th, right after Thanksgiving weekend. Again, because of COVID-19 health protocols, Dave was not allowed to have anyone come inside with him. This meant, for four hours he was connected to an IV doing chemotherapy. This was followed by radiation treatment where he had to sit alone with no one to be with him for moral support. It also meant I had to wait for those four hours alone with the kids. It would have been nice if I could have gone to somebody's house to visit while we waited, but that still wasn't allowed. This meant we waited in the car, walked around Walmart, listened to preschool songs, and played I Spy way too many times. It was exhausting and yet I felt I didn't have anything to complain about. Dave was currently undergoing chemotherapy and radiation treatment for cancer. My exhaustion seemed completely unjustified compared to Dave's cancer treatment.

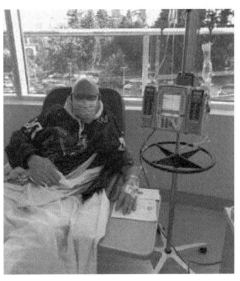

Dave undergoing chemotherapy treatment

Even as I thought about it, I couldn't quite comprehend what was happening. Was this really our life right now? Surprisingly Dave felt okay after the first day of treatment. I've never walked along-side someone so close to me going through cancer treatment. I wasn't sure what to expect. Based on what I see in movies and such, I thought he might be vomiting sick or falling asleep. He felt somewhat normal. For the next three days of the week, he still went to work and drove himself to the Cancer Centre for radiation after work each day. Maybe it's his strong-willed personality or the fact he is extremely stubborn, but he insisted on driving himself on the radiation days if he could, and he insisted he could still work thus far.

Dave's work was amazing. The company was very accommodating, gave him all the tools he needed to make his job easier and told him to only do what he could. He was blessed by having such solid support and a routine.

Meanwhile, I was starting to really struggle. This was all getting harder than I thought it would be. By Halloween, I was losing hope. Sometimes, when I struggle with hope in life, I pack up for the day and head to the town of Hope, about a forty-minute drive away. I got the idea from a friend once, and I do it every so often. There is nothing quite like sitting in the middle of nowhere knowing you are surrounded by Hope. It is just so satisfying.

By the end of the day, it was time to head back home. We had big plans to have dinner at my in-laws and go trick or treating with the kids and all their cousins. This was Jeremiah's first year; he was dressed as a little bear cub. My dad built a cage that fit over our wagon, and we planned to have Jeremiah in the wagon as the captured bear, and Jesse as the police officer who caught him. It was going to be epic!

By the time it was dark and we were all ready to go trick or treating, Jeremiah was clearly ready for bed. This was going to be interesting. I needed him to sit in a seat in the wagon, and all he wanted was to nurse to sleep. We tried and tried to get him to be happy and content, but nothing was working. My anxiety was getting higher and higher, as was the volume of Jeremiah's screaming. By now, kids were out trick-or-treating, and I was ready to lose it.

My anxiety kicked into an all-time high as Dave's friend came to drop off a meal. Dave was too weak to walk around the neighbourhood, and Jesse was excited to go get some candy! A meal was being dropped off and Jeremiah wouldn't stop screaming. What was I going to do? Suddenly I could feel the anxiety boiling over and I knew what was happening, but I couldn't stop it. I was having a panic attack.

I was crying and crying to the point of hyperventilating there on the street in front of all the kids going about their business on Halloween night. Out of desperation, I asked Dave's friend to take Jesse trick or treating for me while my mother-in-law was at the front door calling me inside. The street on Halloween was not the place to be having one of my "moments" I called them.

I took Jeremiah inside, brought him downstairs and got him ready for bed. Through deep breathing and reassuring myself, I was in a safe place, I managed to control my panic attack and bring my breathing back to a normal rate. I felt so defeated; it was our job to be taking Jesse and Jeremiah out. Instead, I was at home missing out on Jesse trick-or-treating, and Jeremiah didn't even get to go.

Normally, I don't think this would bother me as much as it did this year. This was Jeremiah's first Halloween and with Dave undergoing cancer treatment to try and save his life, I was frazzled, to say the least!

CHAPTER 11
NOVEMBER 2020
BREAKING

I honestly don't really remember much of November. I know starting off November, Dave had already had three chemotherapy treatments and 13 radiation treatments. It would have been 14, but one of the sessions had to be skipped because Dave lost too much weight and the radiation mask didn't fit properly. They needed to fit him for a new mask which couldn't be ready until the next day. Unfortunately, due to the absolute need of every session, they had to add one more session onto his end date to make up for this one. When you're facing a terminal diagnosis, there's no risking anything.

As the month of November went on, it was easy to see how quickly Dave's physical strength was diminishing. He was no longer able to work on site, but his work quickly accommodated him with the equipment he needed to do his work from home. His job included doing multiple counts of inventory of everything in the building. From home, although he was not there to physically count products, he could hand out tasks to others in his department as well as enter all the inventory into a spreadsheet on the laptop his work provided him for home use.

It was still difficult for Dave to keep up with work because the exhaustion was more than he had expected, and he just didn't have it in him. He continued working until November 19th and then finally admitted he couldn't do it anymore. He was done. It was hard for him to come to that, but he did amazing. He worked almost full-time for 5 weeks of cancer treatment! No wonder he was so worn already!

At this point, he no longer had the ability to drive, so I drove him to all his radiation treatments in Abbotsford. We were still in the pandemic, and restrictions were still very strict. There was to be no socializing in homes for any reason, or you could get a ticket. Now, here I sat, every single day in the hospital parking lot with our four-month-old baby, waiting for Daddy to have radiation treatment. The cancer centre used to allow family members to come in with the patients, but again, due to COVID-19 protocols, this was no longer allowed. In fact, we were not even allowed to go into the hospital unless we were a patient. So, one day when Jeremiah is older, there will be lots of driver's seat selfies to go through as there really wasn't anything else we could do. Luckily Jeremiah was an easy-going baby and didn't mind too much. And he loved to smile for the camera.

Jeremiah and Mommy driver's seat selfie

The only other place I frequented was Community Services because of the ties I had with the **Best for Babies** program. When I was pregnant with my first son Jesse, I attended the **Best for Babies** program, which was a program run weekly for pregnant moms and moms of new babies. It is meant to be a safe place to come together with other moms on a similar path while also being able to connect with amazing resources and supports like diapers, bottles, formula, counselling, parent courses, parent workshops, as well as bins and bins of donated baby items for moms to pick through. It was the best experience, and I was so thankful for it.

Dave even came with me to the groups and then started

volunteering as "the baby whisperer" after Jesse aged out. When I got pregnant with Jeremiah, I was so thankful I was able to go back to the program. Dave never really left the group. He found as he recovered from his PTSD journey, that snuggling babies was the absolute best therapy. He remained a volunteer until it was shut down due to COVID-19 restrictions.

I did go back to the groups at **Best for Babies** when I got pregnant with Jeremiah, but it stopped running when I was five months pregnant. The staff and other moms there barely even saw my belly bump before everything was shut down. Eventually the group was moved to an online platform, but the doors were always open if someone needed one-on-one help or supplies. I frequented there just to sit and talk. Dave was going through treatments, and I had nothing else to do but sit with my baby. The staff there have been amazing. Throughout my pregnancy with Jesse and Jeremiah, they have become like family to us.

I remember vividly calling Liz at **Best for Babies** one day crying, because I had to peel an egg… I know, it sounds ridiculous. But until this point, Dave was still capable of meeting most of his needs himself other than driving. I was overwhelmed all the time taking care of two kids and the house and trying to process cancer treatment while going through post-partum depression. This one day, Dave made himself a soft-boiled egg to eat. At this time, it was one of the only things he could get down his throat comfortably without it burning. Radiation treatment does that to you. He got his egg and an extra bowl, sat on the couch, and prepared to peel it. I was on the floor struggling with a crying baby who just wanted to be held. After all the energy it took for Dave to make the egg, he was too weak to peel it.

He literally had no physical energy to peel the egg. He would never normally ask me when he knows I am already struggling with Jeremiah, but he did. He hadn't been able to eat in days, and he needed this egg. He looked and me and told me he just couldn't peel it and kindly asked if I would do it for him. Of course, I did. I sat on the floor with my crying baby, peeling his egg while he zoned out to the tv, too weak to do anything else. I fought the tears hard, but they were coming. This was the hardest moment I had faced so far. Either that or this was my breaking point. Either way, I peeled the egg, gave it to Dave, got Jeremiah ready to go, and told Dave I was leaving to go get a coffee before picking up Jesse. As soon as I walked out the door, the tears came streaming down my face. Why was that so hard? It was only an egg. An egg and a crying baby. I never expected this journey to be as hard on me as it was.

By the last week of November, things were getting tough. Dave was no longer able to eat anything, he was going through about 40 Litres of water a week, was losing way too much weight too quickly, and didn't have the strength to keep up. He barely had the strength to stand up and get himself to the bathroom. I was carrying the burden of the home, the boys, and now fully Dave. It was too much for me and I just didn't think I could do it anymore.

By the end of November, Dave could no longer manage at home and needed to be admitted to the hospital. He only had another week of treatment left, but we were told things would continue to get worse before they got better. On November 26th, Dave went to the Abbotsford Hospital for his routine radiation treatment, and it was decided he would be staying there for the duration of his treatment at least, if not more.

Part of me was relieved because there was nothing further I could do for him at home. I knew he needed to be in the hospital being taken care of by medical professionals, but at the same time I was heartbroken and crushed. I didn't dare complain about me, considering what Dave was going through, but here I was now at home with my two young children in the middle of a pandemic with no help while Daddy is in the hospital fighting cancer. I could not believe this was my life — heading into Christmas time, no doubt.

Dave went into the hospital on a Thursday, and by the weekend, I was stretched beyond my capabilities. I had a sleepover planned for Jesse with his Auntie Shelley and Uncle Luke. I needed some time to think, and I hadn't been sleeping. It was best for Jesse if he spent a good portion of the weekend getting extra positive attention from some family. I didn't have it in me to be positive all day and night. During the week was one thing, because Jesse went to daycare, so I had the daytime hours to journal or write or talk to a friend. Over the weekend, I just had a very needy three-year-old all day.

I felt weak to say I couldn't do it alone and needed help, but I've realized it is in fact, strength. It is strength to stand up and ask for help. It is strength to admit you are struggling. For me to reach my full potential as a parent, I need to be able to admit where I am struggling and need help. This is what allows me to move forward. This is what allows me to take care of some of my needs, as we all need to do from time to time.

Driving Jesse to Luke and Shelley's was exciting and hard. Jesse had never been away from home for a sleepover before. Even when we were in the hospital having Jeremiah,

Jesse was still at home. He went upstairs to spend part of the day with Grandma and Papa, and later, my friend Jordan came with her daughter Emma and slept over. So, he has never slept away from home. Luckily for me, he was looking forward to it. He loves his Auntie Shelley and Uncle Luke. It may have helped that Uncle Luke almost always had candy for him!

Once we got there, Jesse was happy to go in and look all around their new house. They had recently moved since the last time we had been to their house. It took him no time to ask Auntie Shelley, "Do you have a couple of toys for me to play with?" I knew he would be totally fine there. It was still hard to leave though especially knowing I was only leaving him because I needed some time, space, and a break.

I think I still cried all the way home. My emotions were strong from everything happening; I broke. I finally felt free to break and let it out. I often do that when I drive. Even with Jeremiah in the car, I feel free to talk to God and be as loud as I need to. Driving in the car, especially through farmland, is my best place for lashing out and telling God how I feel. It's a safe place for me to break down, cry, scream, yell, whatever I need to do. Jeremiah was such a calm baby. It didn't matter what I needed to do, he let me do it.

When I got home that afternoon after dropping Jesse off, I settled quickly, and took a breath. All I needed to do was put Jeremiah to bed and the house would finally be quiet. Jeremiah went down easy at 6 o'clock and then I just sat there. I didn't know what to do with myself. I was always being pulled either between two kids or household chores, but I did all the right things to set myself up for success. I cleaned the house earlier, picked up dinner on my way home, and had a glass of wine ready to go for when Jeremiah was down for the night. I needed this, and I was ready.

I honestly don't remember how the evening went by so quickly. I spent some time writing, sometime praying, and fell asleep early. Not nearly as exciting as I had hoped, but I was exhausted both mentally and physically, I needed rest. I was looking forward to sleeping past 5 o'clock the next morning. Jeremiah slept with me in our bed, so if I was near him he would stay sleeping for quite some time. It was Jesse who was always the early riser, sometimes even before 5am. It was exhausting even on a good day.

The next day was Sunday, and I had church to look forward to — sort of. This was the first Sunday Dave was not with me for church. Since churches were closed and moved online in March, we had been together for every single one from the centre of our living room. Jesse had the choice of watching with us or playing in his room quietly. Every time he went running down the hall, we would look at each other and say, "Oh, Jesse is going to Sunday school now." After Jeremiah was born, he sat with either Dave or I and watched with us (or slept). Either way, we were all together, every time, until now.

On this day I was watching church alone with Jeremiah. Jesse wasn't there interrupting, and Dave wasn't there turning the volume up over Jesse's tablet. It was just on. It felt weird. I was used to the chaos as chaotic as that sounds. When church was over, and Jeremiah had napped, we left to go pick up Jesse from Luke and Shelley's. I missed Jesse. Shelley kept me posted through text messages though, so I knew he had done well, thank goodness.

As I got to the door, Jesse came running. He was so

excited to see me. It made my day and melted my heart. I knew he would miss me, but this was a big run into my arms hug. If you know Jesse at all, he is not a hugger. He is not a touchy-feely person at all. In fact, if you ask him for a hug, he'll sort of do this lean in thing and let you hug him, but he won't quite give the hug. This day though, I got the best Jesse hug there ever was. I was happy to have him back in my arms.

I had a good break and felt rejuvenated. I got Jesse home, played in his room for a while, and got ready for dinner, bath, and bed. The next day was a daycare day, and even though Dave wasn't back yet, things needed to return to a somewhat normal standard for Jesse's sake.

The next day, I vividly remember how hard the rain was pouring. It was still dark when I brought Jesse to daycare. Rain had been falling hard throughout the night and was just starting to ease off. I got home, unbuckled Jeremiah, and proceeded to walk the 15 steps down the outside of the house to our basement suite entrance out back. As I got to the door, the sun rose and shone just the right way on something shiny in the garden beside my door.

As I bent down, I couldn't believe my eyes. It appeared to be an engagement ring smothered in dirt. I couldn't tell if it was real or not, but how bizarre to find an engagement ring in the dirt outside my front door. It must have fallen off someone's finger recently. I brought it inside and washed it off. Looking at it, it looked real to me but who in the world could it belong to?

Trying to track down an owner would take me forever. Recently we had so many people coming by to bring us a meal, a coffee, groceries, or something else we needed.

Our network of friends and family has been outrageously supportive and helpful, which was amazing, but that meant I had a lot of tracking down to do. First, I took it to the jewellers to determine if it was in fact a real diamond, and sure enough, it was!

A friend of ours started an online food train for us where people could sign up and drop off meals to us. It was a huge help as we were so stressed out just trying to function during the day, let alone feed ourselves healthy, nutritious food. The meal train kicked off and before we knew it, we had someone bringing us a meal every other night at least. Because of the food train, we not only had support in meals and prayers, but I was reconnecting with a lot of old friends. I reconnected with high school friends who are now having babies, friends from our church who I didn't know very well, and friends from my early childhood.

During one of the times, my friend Kate came to bring me something, we got talking outside. She was now pregnant with her second child, and it was exciting to talk about how much we had in common with each other now. She only had a few weeks left to go of her pregnancy, and so I asked her what the toughest thing has been. She told me it was probably her memory. I laughed as I could very easily remember just how dumb I felt in pregnancy. I called it pregnancy brain and I felt just clueless. I asked Kate what her best (or worst) pregnancy brain moment was. She responded by saying, "I've been losing everything from my earrings, my engagement ring, my…" I think I heard her right. I had to clarify. Again, she told me she lost her engagement ring. It had been too big for her finger, and she kept meaning to get it sized but kept forgetting and now she was really wishing she had. I asked if she could describe what her ring looked like and as she described it, my face lit up. I couldn't believe what I was hearing. I ran inside, grabbed the ring that I had found in the dirt, and ran it out. Kate's face lit up! It was her ring — the engagement ring she had lost. It must have fallen off her finger one day she was here dropping off a meal for us. How amazing that I was able to not only reconnect with her but to reunite her with her ring and have this be part of our story.

CHAPTER 12
DECEMBER 2020
A LONELY CHRISTMAS

December 3rd was an exciting day as it was the last day of Dave's cancer treatment. Because of COVID-19, family members were not allowed in with patients during treatment, but the hospital did make an exception for Dave's last radiation appointment. I was able to go see him and be there with him for his last treatment. I was so excited to see Dave that day! I dropped Jesse off at his daycare first thing in the morning and headed into Abbotsford. It had only been a week since I had seen Dave, but it seemed like so much longer.

I met my sister-in-law out front of the hospital so she could watch Jeremiah for a bit while I was with Dave. It was too much for me, both physically and emotionally, to have to deal with Jeremiah while also finally being able to spend a few minutes with Dave celebrating this amazing victory. Jeremiah was still only five months old and required lots of time and attention. Karen took him for a walk to Starbucks and had some good auntie/nephew bonding time.

Once Karen was off with Jeremiah in the stroller, I threw on my mask and walked (maybe skipped) into the doors of the Cancer Centre waiting to finally see my husband after this long week. I checked in at the desk, went to the elevator, and proceeded to go down to ground zero of the hospital where Dave would be having his final radiation treatment. When I got downstairs, I waited.

I sat there anxiously tapping my foot and looking all around, desperate to finally see my husband. Finally, I saw them wheel him toward me. My heart skipped a beat as I saw him wheel closer and closer to me. It had only been a week, but it felt so much longer. To finally be here with him, to be able to hold him and hug him, felt amazing. Together, we went down the hall to radiation and waited for him to be called in to his very last session.

Radiation treatment was nothing like I ever expected it to be. I didn't really know anything about it before or how it was done, for that matter. Through Dave's treatment, he had told me about it, but I hadn't seen anything until this day. We walked into the radiation room and there in the middle of the room was a small table for the patient to lay on and a massive radiation machine. The rest of the room was full of various pieces of medical equipment and screens of information regarding the radiation equipment and the patient. I walked as Dave was wheeled over to the table. I watched as they helped Dave up onto the little table and positioned his body in just the right spot. It was very important to lay in the exact right spot and not move because the radiation is targeted at specific areas where the cancer is. To do this, Dave had to wear this fitted, hard white mask over his face. It was screwed to the table to ensure he couldn't move his head even a little bit. There was a ball that had to be placed in his mouth beforehand and a band to hold his hands together.

It did not look comfortable. I couldn't believe Dave had done this 35 times, for the last seven weeks. He was amazing and so strong for going through all that. I was so proud of him.

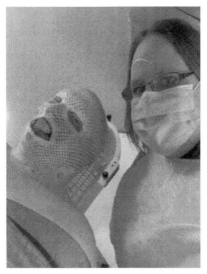

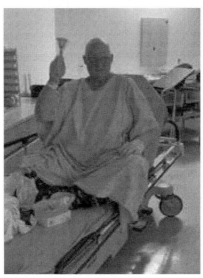

Dave's last day of radiation!

Unfortunately, after his treatment, he had to go back up to the oncology ward where they would not allow visitors. I had to then say my goodbyes to Dave until the day he was well enough to come home. According to the doctors, the effects of the radiation treatment, although done, would continue to worsen for the next two weeks. He already couldn't eat, walk, or talk. How much worse could it get?

One of the hardest things about this time was Dave losing the ability to talk. It was hard enough with him not being able to be here, but now we couldn't even talk on the phone. Texting, as much as it was my main platform of communication, was too difficult for me at that time because I was struggling with tennis elbow. I'm not even sure what that is, but my hands, wrists, and arms hurt all the time. I could barely hold my phone without feeling excruciating pain, let alone type a message. And yet, this was the only way Dave, and I could communicate. We would Face-Time quite a bit so he could see the kids, but he couldn't talk, so it was only good for me to talk and him to see the boys. It really wasn't the same as him being here.

I can't tell you how many times my heart just sank because something came to mind, and I wanted to tell him, but he wasn't there. Whether it was something new Jeremiah did or something funny Jesse said, or something blonde and dumb I did, I just missed his presence so much. Even doing laundry made me miss him. By the second week of December, he had been in the hospital for two weeks. There were no longer any of his clothes in circulation to fold and put away. Who knew laundry could make someone so sad?

As December went on, the days all blurred together. I was missing Dave so much while also losing my mind at home. Because of the pandemic, Dave was not allowed to have any visitors. I could not go see him, and he couldn't see his kids except over Face-Time. It was awful. Dave's mental health started to decline as did mine. Jesse and Jeremiah must have picked up on the tension too because their mood and behaviours were especially unsettled.

It was getting tough doing it alone at home. I know under normal circumstances, I would have significantly more physical support, but again, because of COVID-19 and current restrictions in place, we were not allowed visitors in our home. I needed more help at home, but it wasn't allowed, and I think that was the most frustrating part for me. I remember one night, a couple of family members came by to drop off a meal for me. It was very much appreciated but when they were at my door, I was losing my mind. It was dingbat hour as I liked to call it, and the kids were driving me mental. When I opened the door, I asked out of desperation if they could please come in just for a few minutes and help me. They politely declined, telling me it wasn't safe because of the virus.

I don't know if I had ever felt so alone. This was family and yet it still wasn't safe for them to come in. I politely thanked them for the meal, closed the door, and broke down crying. I didn't feel like I had the strength to keep going. It wasn't just being the single parent that broke me, it was the emotional toll it was taking on me mentally thinking about Dave and why he wasn't with me. It was the fact that the kids were also missing Daddy and confused as to why he wasn't here. It was wondering how much worse this was going to get. And finally, it was wondering if the treatment was even going to work. Was this going to be for nothing, or would it be worth all this? It was not something I wanted to think about and yet it was a thought that never left my head.

I looked forward to Thursday evenings, the one day a week where I had help. Liz from **Best for Babies** volunteered her time to come out and help me during dingbat hour. She wore a mask and we kept physical distance, but she was here. I can't tell you how much that meant to me to have someone here. Whether it was someone for me to talk to or someone to just sit in Jesse's room with the kids while I try and think straight for a minute or make dinner or unpack Jesse's lunch, it was amazing. I had her support to help me get through the dinner hour and bedtime for the kids.

After this, I realized how much I absolutely needed this support, this hands-on physical support. I wondered if there could be a loophole in the system for my mental health. I called my psychiatrist's office to inquire as I had an idea that just might work. I asked about him writing a letter for me to keep by my door stating I can have someone in my home for medical reasons. He was not only happy to do it but was proud of me for coming up with such a great and unique idea. I still had to follow all the public health orders such as wearing a mask and physical distance, but this was my ticket for help. It was so unfortunate we were in this time, and this is what it took for me to have someone come hold my baby, but I was so thankful!

During Dave's stay at the hospital, he had another surgery done to insert a feeding tube into his stomach. He could no longer eat or drink anything, and he was losing significantly too much weight. When he first got the feeding tube, he was on a formula drip which ran all day. The nurses took care of it, and Dave didn't need to worry about anything. It was good for him to just rest and focus on healing and getting better. When he did come home though, he would need to know how to properly use the feeding tube. The nurses and dieticians at the hospital felt it would be best if he also had one or two other people to come to the hospital to take a short lesson on the feeding tube and how it worked.

My mother-in-law and I drove in together to learn how to use and change the feeding tube. Jeremiah accompanied us of course. I remember feeling so split in the middle. I was excited to finally see Dave but to learn how to feed him through a feeding tube! I remember vividly being in the room with Dave, my mother-in-law, the dietician, myself, Jeremiah, and a few other ladies who were there to learn as well. As I watched the dietician show us how to do all the ins and outs of tube feeding, Jeremiah needed to nurse. I tried to distract him to buy myself some time, but he was adamant he wanted milk now. I found a seat in the room and sat down to nurse him while quietly watching and listening to the dietician's instructions. I tried so hard to focus, but I was feeling so overwhelmed. I was so thankful my mother-in-law was there as well because I honesty wasn't sure how much I was even taking in. I was currently sitting in a chair breastfeeding my baby while learning how to tube feed my husband. That is just not an experience I ever saw myself having in a million years. I think I'm still processing the weirdness of it.

One Friday morning in the second week of December, Dave called me to say he was being discharged.

Honestly, I was a little shocked. I didn't realize that was part of the plan. Based on what I saw on Face-Time, he didn't seem in any condition to come home. Regardless, Dave was insistent he was being discharged, and I could go pick him up. I was hesitant but I missed him so much. I grabbed Jeremiah, changed his diaper, got in the SUV, and headed to Abbotsford. I was so excited to see Dave and have him finally come home. As I pulled out the stroller to put Jeremiah in, Dave texted me to tell me I needed to bring up a wheelchair and wheel him down. Well, I wasn't sure how I would pull that off, but I honestly wasn't thinking. I just headed straight to the main doors with Jeremiah in the stroller. Maybe I could push one and pull one?

As I walked into the doors of the Abbotsford Regional Hospital and Cancer Centre, there were two women waiting at a desk to see where you were going and if you had any signs of COVID-19. I told them I was there to pick up my husband, but I needed to bring a wheelchair and wasn't quite sure how to manage. One of the girls said she would gladly go up and grab Dave for me and bring him down. She told me to go grab our vehicle and come to the front door and she would wheel him down and out front for me. So, Jeremiah and I walked back to the SUV, and drove to the front. We waited for some time, but Dave wasn't coming out. I wasn't sure what I should do but then I received a very upsetting text from Dave saying he wasn't going home today. I was finally able to go visit him though!

Upon entering the hospital again, the same two women were there, and they said Dave was not ready to come home but I was able to go up and see him. I went to the elevators with Jeremiah in the stroller and headed to the oncology ward. When I got to the front desk and told the staff who I was, they instantly filled me in. A nurse got me to follow her down the hall as she explained to me what happened. Apparently, Dave had asked to be discharged even though the nurses did not feel he was ready. They tried to explain to him he wasn't ready, but he was insistent he was. They decided at first they would take his word and allow him to be discharged because he was so desperate to just go home. Upon standing up, though, he just about passed out. At that point, the nurses there made a final decision he was in fact, not yet ready to come home.

Because Dave was so upset, the nurses at the hospital allowed me to come in and see him. They normally were not allowing visitors, but they gave me an open pass because of the state of Dave's mental health. It was Christmas time, and he was just missing his family so much. This just seemed so unfair. As I walked into his hospital room, I could clearly see how not ready he was. He looked so worn out and just absolutely done. He couldn't even stand up. He wanted to hold Jeremiah, but he was even too weak to do that. I was able to lean Jeremiah against Dave for a quick picture, but I could not leave him there and walk away. That part was hard. Just a year earlier, Dave had been a volunteer at the **Best for Babies** program and often had two, if not three babies in his hands. At one point, we even got a photo of him holding five babies. Seeing him too weak to hold his own baby, even sitting, was tough.

Dave trying to hold Jeremiah in the hospital

After seeing Dave, I headed back home with an empty front seat and an empty heart. Even if he wasn't yet ready to come home, I was certainly ready for him to be home. By this point, I had been a single parent for 16 days and to say we missed him at home was an understatement. I was exhausted, worn out, I had nothing left in me, and yet I had to keep going. I had two young kids at home, depending on me to parent them, regardless of what was happening with their dad.

Over that weekend, while Dave was in the hospital, he focussed hard on recovering so he could come home. By Monday, the nurses and doctors were all in agreement that if Dave really felt ready, he could go home. I was so excited! It had been nearly three weeks since he was at home and as much as I didn't know what to expect, I knew I just needed him home with me.

*Jeremiah photo bombing our selfie
on the day Dave gets to leave the hospital*

Once I got to the hospital and saw Dave, my mind went two ways. First place it went was straight to my heart where I missed him so incredibly much. I just wanted him to be back home with me so bad. I didn't care about anything else. But then, as I thought about it and looked at Dave and the condition he was in, I realized this was going to be a lot of work. He was still shaky on his feet, he needed tons of medications throughout the day, his feeding tube needed to be run through and washed out three times a day, and Dave's current capabilities were limited to sitting and resting.

I remember that first Monday he was home. I think I did 25 flights of stairs that day. We lived in the basement suite of my in-laws and to help me out, Dave was going to stay upstairs for the first few days where his mom and dad could help as well. It was truly a blessing to have someone with whom to share the responsibilities. Between crushing pills, measuring liquid medication, cleaning feeding tube bags, and running what he needed upstairs, I was exhausted. Luckily Jesse was at daycare, so I just had to have Jeremiah with me, but that meant I was doing 25 flights of stairs hauling everything everywhere with my 20-pound five-month-old on my back. After a couple days, I was absolutely done physically, emotionally, and mentally.

By Wednesday morning, the 16th of December, I felt like I just wanted to run away. I felt terrible for thinking that, but I was so exhausted. I've had two kids and done the newborn stage twice, and yet I have never felt exhaustion quite like this before. I was done and yet it had only been two days of Dave being home. It's not that I wanted him back in the hospital, I just wanted him well. Seeing him struggle to do everything was the most difficult thing I have gone through in our marriage thus far. All I wanted to do was get in the car and drive. The Archway Community Services in Abbotsford had put together some Christmas gift bags for the kids of families that had been a part of the **Best for Babies** program and the Family Centre for the past while. They had contacted me to see about picking up my bag. Since I needed out of the house, I figured this would be a great way for me to do something productive, see my community services family, and get a break from home as bad as that sounded.

I remember driving out to Abbotsford with Jeremiah. Luckily, Jesse was at daycare again. I was so tired, both physically and mentally, I almost didn't feel present driving out there. I knew I was driving on the freeway but honestly,

I felt so dazed and confused, I probably shouldn't have been driving at all. Thankfully, I made it safely. I parked my van, got out Jeremiah and walked up the stairs. Most of the staff were there at the top of the stairs at a table handing out the gift bags. As I walked up the stairs, I don't even remember what happened next. I just remember walking up the stairs and then I remember sitting on the couch inside. I guess one of the staff asked if I wanted to come in; I'm not sure.

I remember breaking down out of exhaustion because I did not feel strong enough to take this on. Why had God given me so much? And why was I even complaining about me? Dave was the one who went through the treatment. It shouldn't even be about me. I was just so tired and worn out, I couldn't think straight. At one point, while Cindy was holding Jeremiah, I laid down on the couch because I was just too tired to sit up. Before I knew it, I was passed out asleep on the couch in the middle of the room. Cindy went on and did a whole prenatal group call over zoom with Jeremiah on her lap while I slept and slept. I woke up shocked I had even fallen asleep and honestly a little embarrassed. I was so worn out though, I must have needed it.

This was the time of year where normally people would be hosting Christmas parties, end-of-year parties, family get-togethers, school Christmas productions, work Christmas events, community Christmas events, all things Christmas. This year, all those things were cancelled. Province-wide restrictions were still in place banning gatherings of any size even in our home. That meant not only were the large community, school, and work events cancelled, but as was any hope of having family together for Christmas. Restrictions in place stated there could be no inside gatherings of any kind. Whether it was play dates with friends, a coffee visit, or Christmas dinner, it didn't matter.

As hard as it was to prepare for Christmas knowing there wouldn't be an official family Christmas dinner, it was nice knowing Dave was back with me. And my in-laws lived upstairs, and so we were able to plan a dinner together since we live in the same household. We were all so worn though. Dave was still recovering on the couch or in bed, I was so worn out from taking care of everyone and preparing for Christmas, my mother-in-law had thrown her back out, and my father-in-law was starting to have some health issues. Here we were allowed to be together for a Christmas dinner and yet none of us had it in us to make a Christmas dinner.

It was like God answered our prayers because as I scrolled through Facebook one day, I saw a post from a lovely woman looking for a way to bless the community. She and her husband were planning on making a giant turkey dinner and then delivering it to ten different families in the Chilliwack area. They wanted to spread some Christmas cheer during a time when it seemed the world had lost all its own. I contacted this family to see about arranging to make her list. I explained our situation, and she was happy to include us in this wonderful giving project. I was so thankful for this person reaching out to try and help other families in our community.

Before we knew it, it was Christmas Eve. Not a Christmas Eve we were normally used to but a Christmas Eve, nonetheless. There wasn't a Christmas Eve church service, Christmas Eve get together, or anything Christmas happening but we were together. Considering the year, we had just had, I was more than content to just be together here in our home for Christmas. Dave was very slowly getting better and better each day. By this point he was talking a little better, sleeping a little less, and could go up and down the stairs about once a day. He was also now able to swallow one of his medications he needed. Before this, he had to open the capsule, crush up all the small pieces, mix it with some water, and insert it into his feeding tube. It was an ordeal to say the least. For Dave to be able to swallow a pill, it was an amazing milestone!

The only issue we were facing now was his feeding tube. Over the course of a few days, the feeding tube was giving him some issues with clogging. He was given a kit with some instructions on what to do if it clogs, and he tried that, but it just kept happening. I wondered if we should maybe have it checked out, but Dave was so fearful of being admitted into the hospital, he didn't want to go back there. He had just spent three weeks there alone, away from his family. It was Christmas time now and although it was a Christmas unlike any other, we needed to be together.

On the morning of Christmas Eve, Dave's feeding tube was having issues again. We were able to unclog it, but I was starting to get concerned. By the afternoon, it was clogged again and this time there was a small pimple-like bump forming about an inch beside where the feeding tube was inserted. It could have been coincidence, but my gut told me to keep an eye on it. By 4 o'clock that day, the pimple like bump had not only tripled in size, but the contents from Dave's current feeding tube bag was slowly dripping out of that bump. His food was literally going in one hole and coming out another and I was watching it happen.

I knew what we had to do but I couldn't face it. It was

Christmas Eve. I knew Dave needed medical attention now, but I didn't want to spend our Christmas Eve waiting for Dave in emergency. We didn't have a choice though, Dave needed help. My in laws were currently dropping off gifts for the other grandkids so we had to take both kids. I was trying to figure out what to do with both kids while we wait for Dave. Of course, because of COVID-19, we couldn't go visit inside anyone's home, we also could not enter the hospital unless we were patients, and because it was Christmas Eve, almost everything was closed. I couldn't even grab myself a coffee at a drive-through, it was so depressing.

As I didn't know what to do with the kids, I decided to bring some of the wrapped presents with us so they could at least have something fun to do in the van while we waited. I can't tell you how much my heart sunk to load my children into the vehicle to bring Daddy to the hospital yet again, this time on a day when we should all be together. We were already apart from the rest of our family because of the virus, now my kids were away from their father, and I was away from my husband.

As we were driving out to the Abbotsford hospital, Dave called his parents to let them know what was happening. They were on their way back home from Abbotsford, so they offered to meet us halfway and pick up Jesse and bring him back home. I didn't want to be away from Jesse either, but I also didn't want him to have to sit in a vehicle for who knows how long this would take, maybe hours. We met halfway and passed off Jesse as well as the gifts we had brought with us. I couldn't leave Jeremiah quite yet as he was still strictly breastfed, and I didn't know how long we would be.

After we dropped off Jesse, we proceeded to head to the hospital. I dropped off Dave out front of emergency, and went for a drive. I was amazed to see how quiet the city was. By this time, it was after 5:00 pm on Christmas Eve. No one was out, and nothing was open; it felt like a dead city. I ended up driving around and around and eventually back to the hospital parking lot with Jeremiah while I waited for some news. Eventually, Dave was seen, and it was determined for sure there was not only an infection, but the feeding tube had become dislodged. The only thing they could do was pull it out and schedule a surgery for a new one. This required a certain type of surgeon, and that specific surgeon was not working weekends and holidays. It was Christmas Eve... on a Thursday night!

Because Christmas Eve fell on Thursday, that meant the next business day was Tuesday. Monday became a holiday in lieu of Boxing Day on Saturday. Dave could not be released home with no way to consume calories so that meant he had to stay in the hospital on IV fluids from Christmas Eve until after he had another feeding tube put it. I couldn't believe what I was hearing. I now had to drive back home on Christmas Eve, leaving my husband behind at the hospital. When I got home, Jesse was tucked into bed at Grandma and Papa's house for a sleepover. One of his gifts was new Paw Patrol bedding and since it had gotten so late, it was better for Jesse to get tucked into bed there.

Christmas Eve wrapped up by me crawling into bed by myself with just Jeremiah beside me. This was Jeremiah's first Christmas, and he and I were all alone. It just didn't seem right. This time last year I wondered what our first Christmas would look like as a family of four. This is certainly not what I pictured. It was crazy how much can change in just a year.

Waking up Christmas morning was lonely and depressing. I leaned over to wish my baby his first Merry Christmas and quickly realized, that other than him, I was alone. I missed Dave so much. It just didn't seem fair he was waking up on Christmas morning in the hospital, and I was waking up without him. We have never been apart for Christmas since the day we met. In fact, our first Christmas together was when Dave proposed to me. He gave me all my presents and then had this last one in a tall slim box. I never would have thought there would be an engagement ring at the bottom, but sure enough, under all that tissue paper, there was a ring and his proposal. I will never forget the feeling of that first Christmas together.

Here we are now on our ninth Christmas together, only not together. The weight in my stomach seemed to only get heavier as I remembered Jesse had his first sleepover upstairs. I knew it was only a matter of walking upstairs to see him, but it wasn't the same as waking up to having him right near me, excited for the Christmas festivities to begin. I wasn't ready to go upstairs yet, I needed more time. I needed more time to process this insanity that was happening. I needed to have a coffee and try to think straight. I still had to change Jeremiah's diaper and nurse him. I still had to get dressed and figure out how I was going to do this day without Dave.

I called Dave as soon as I was functioning a bit better. I wanted to be strong for him, but I missed him so much, it was hard. Face-Timing my husband on Christmas Day didn't even come close to meeting the need I had to be with him. I couldn't even imagine what it was like for him. Under normal circumstances, if someone is in the hospital over

Christmas, then family and friends can visit the patient, but we were not in normal times. It had now been over nine months of the pandemic and there wasn't any hope of restrictions loosening up any time soon. Dave would have to be alone in the hospital with no visitors able to see him. And there was no hope of him leaving until after he got another surgery which wouldn't be until at least the 29th.

Being home with two kids, the day carried on as usual. Life doesn't stop even when your heart is torn. I grabbed my coffee and my baby and headed upstairs to see Jesse. Luckily for me, Jesse at 3 years-old was more excited to see me on Christmas morning than get into his presents. I can't tell you how much that warmed my heart. The last thing I wanted to do was get into opening presents without Dave here. But I certainly did need snuggles from my boy. I had some coffee with my in-laws, gave them an update on Dave, and then headed downstairs as Jesse was excited to go back home and play.

I was happy to come back downstairs but I also felt more alone than ever. This was Christmas. Christmas in the pandemic when the whole world is with only their household families; except Dave. Dave was in the hospital alone. It just didn't seem fair. I try not to be a pessimist; in fact, I am usually the opposite. I generally try to keep my head thinking in tough situations like "What could God be showing me through this?", "What am I meant to learn here?", "How can I grow more in this situation?" On this day though, I just didn't feel it in me. My heart had sunk so low, I just couldn't find any reasoning in this.

The day went on as a normal day; we didn't do presents. I let Jesse open one present and then told him the rest would be when Daddy gets home. He seemed content with that, and as young as he was, it's not like he had many other memories to compare to. So, we had a "normal" day, as normal as what normal could be in our household this season. We played in Jesse's room, had breakfast, watched a show, played some more, had lunch and off for naps they went. I probably should have slept too, because I was so sleep deprived, but my brain wouldn't shut off. I missed Dave so much, even my body felt the anxiety.

After nap time was done, we went upstairs to see Grandma and Papa again. Thanks to the turkey dinner we were receiving from the Facebook group, we only had to wait for our drop-off time which was 3:30 pm. Until then, it was a completely normal day. We tried to be as joyful as we could, but it was just so hard. There was no smell of turkey cooking, and no other family around. Now we were doing this without Dave as well.

I don't think I took one photo that day. I didn't want to have physical memories of that Christmas. It's not one I want to look back at often. I just wanted the day to be over. I wanted the kids to go to bed so I could go to bed and not think about Christmas anymore. By the end of the day, I was finding all the Merry Christmas emails, messages, and posts too overwhelming. Most people struggled with this day and yet people still reached out. It meant a lot to me, but I didn't have it in me to even answer a message. In fact, I deactivated my Facebook account without any explanation to anyone around me. I just shut it down and "ran away" from social media.

By the time I woke up on Boxing Day, I thought this would start getting easier, but it wasn't. I seemed to lose the ability to function as a normal, capable, functioning adult in society, let alone a mother of two kids missing their father. I know this is such a negative message to tell myself, but I felt like I couldn't do it anymore. I didn't want to say that in front of Jesse though, because I can only imagine how scary that would sound to a child. I am currently the one person taking care of his every need and for him to hear me say "I can't do it anymore" would probably traumatize him. But I honestly felt like it was true. I needed help.

I called my friend of 13 years who lived about an hour away from me. I was desperate and I knew she not only had a big enough house, but she was familiar with the sensory disorder Jesse had. Her son had the same disorder, so she was very aware to watch for things like tags on a shirt, the white on an orange slice, the end of the pepperoni stick, the need for clean, dry clothes, and the list goes on. Jesse has some unique needs, and they get tricky sometimes if you aren't aware of the things that trigger him. I desperately needed help and as I hoped, Amanda said no problem. So, we packed a bag for Jesse and off we drove to Mission for him to have a sleepover with his friend Kimmie, Amanda's youngest daughter at the time.

As I drove into her driveway, the feeling that arose was not the same as what I normally feel when I see Amanda. We've been friends for so long, it's always good to see her. It's not that it wasn't good to see her today, but I was here to give myself a much-needed toddler break. I love Jesse so much and I want the absolute best for him. Unfortunately, I just had not been in a place well enough to give him my absolute best. He was going to stay and have a sleepover at Amanda's house while I went home and attempted to recharge my emotional battery. Amanda was more than happy to take him despite the current covid restrictions. I guess technically, sleepovers with friends were not allowed, but, in my opinion, this was an essential service I desperately needed beyond belief.

I went inside and got Jesse situated and showed him where he would be sleeping. Thankfully he had been to Amanda's house numerous times, so he was comfortable both with Amanda and her family, as well as her home. Because it was the day after Christmas, the kids there had all new toys they had just unwrapped. Jesse was in heaven, and I was at peace. I felt like I had made the right decision to get this break and try to catch up with all the swirling thoughts happening inside my head. Maybe I might get some sleep too. I still had Jeremiah, as he was still only six months old, but he was a pretty content baby. If I gave him milk and a smile, he was happy. He didn't talk either, so that was a bonus!

The next two days were bittersweet. Jesse ended up spending two nights at Amanda's house. I missed him like crazy, but my anxiety was so bad that driving to the back roads of Mission seemed so daunting. I just didn't feel I was able to handle the drive there and back. Amanda kindly said she would keep Jesse another night as he was having such a good time with his friend Kimmie. I needed another night to try and process the reality that was our life right now. It was still only Saturday, and Dave had no hope of being home until at least Wednesday or Thursday.

By Sunday morning, I had gotten two days to sleep past 5 am, was able to watch church, and was missing Jesse. As soon as I walked in the door at Amanda's house, Jesse came running into my arms. He did just fine and was so good but obviously, he missed me. I felt bad for needing a break, but I knew I would be a better parent if I had it. I have dealt with mental health long enough; I have become quite good at being self-aware and realizing what my needs are. I needed this break, and I was glad I took it. After we collected all of Jesse's belongings, we said our goodbyes to Amanda and her kids and headed to the vehicle. Buckling the kids in, I felt ready to go home. We had made it this far, hopefully it wouldn't be much longer. Dave was hopefully able to have the feeding tube surgery the next day, Tuesday the 29th and if all went well, he could potentially go home 24 hours later.

    I would say Tuesday came quick but really the days were dragging slower than ever. And Tuesday only meant Dave was having yet another surgery, not that he was coming home. That would be Wednesday if we were lucky. Today was just another day; oh and my birthday.

    I missed all the birthday posts and messages from Facebook because I had my account deactivated. But I got some special texts throughout the day. I honestly didn't feel up to doing much that day. At 9 o'clock in the morning, I was preparing to go out for breakfast with my in-laws and noticed my windows on the SUV were frozen and needed to be scraped. I remember thinking it was so much work. I wished so badly Dave was here because he always did this kind of thing for me. He always did it, so I didn't have to do it myself with the two kids. But here I was, alone on my birthday, doing this by myself.

    After breakfast, the rest of the day was a normal day. We played in Jesse's room, had nap/quiet time, played in Jesse's room some more, and watched a couple of shows. I didn't really want to think about my birthday. This whole season was so depressing, this day was too. By the end of the day, Liz came by and brought me sushi for dinner and boy, was I so thankful! All I had to worry about now was getting the kids to bed and I had made it through the day.

We all held our breath in anticipation the next day, anxiously wondering if Dave would be able to come home that day. We waited all day and were starting to lose hope. Finally, not until after 4 pm, did they give the okay for Dave to go home. Finally, after another long week of being separated, through Christmas no less, we were finally going to be back together. Dave got home around six o'clock and we got to be together as a family again.

I can't tell you how good it felt to have him home in my arms. And he looked good too. Obviously, he was still recovering from treatment and was nowhere near 100%, but he looked and seemed a whole lot better than he did when we dropped him off at the hospital. The fact he walked down the outside stairs and still stood for a minute with a smile on his face, told me how much stronger he was. I was so proud of him and so happy he was home. Now we could get on with life and celebrate Christmas as the family of four we were.

The next day, although New Year's Eve, was truly Christmas for us. We had been sponsored by a couple of families this year and had significantly more than our normal number of gifts. I hadn't exactly had it in me to focus on Christmas shopping and wrapping this year, so I was and am eternally grateful to these families! Because we were so blessed, we decided to break it up throughout the day. We did some gifts in the morning, and then went upstairs to visit my in-laws. Then we did a few more and took a break to clean up the mess and play with some new toys. Jesse had a blast going up and down the new slide that he and Jeremiah got, and Jeremiah was honestly happiest with a piece of wrapping paper on the floor. By evening, we had finished up all our unwrapping and finally took a breath.

Sitting there at the end of the day was a little bit surreal. Looking back at New Year's Eve last year, who knew we would deal with cancer twice and a global pandemic? It was just crazy to think of where a year could take us. Now here we were with absolutely no idea what the next year held. Did the cancer treatment work? Would Dave be cancer free or given a terminal diagnosis? Would we continue being a family of four (or even five or six one day) or would I be a single parent in a couple years due to Dave's death? All these thoughts kept flooding my head. All I did to ground myself was hang onto the verse Jeremiah 29:11, "For I know the plans I have for you, declares the Lord, plans to prosper you and not to harm you, plans to give you a hope and a future." Whatever the next year would bring, I trusted it was part of God's plan.

CHAPTER 13

JANUARY 2021

A NEW YEAR

January 1st started off another year. This time, I think the whole world was on edge; everyone was exhausted from the pandemic. The high hopes for a good year seemed to have vanished after the last year we just had, not just for our family but for the rest of the world too. There were no New Year's parties, few New Year's posts and texts compared to previous years, and overall, it was just another day.

I tried not to think ahead of this whole year. Sometime within the next couple of months, Dave would have a PET scan to determine if the cancer treatment was successful. We already knew if it wasn't, Dave would then be given a terminal diagnosis. It was not something I wanted to think about, but it wouldn't leave my mind. The only thing I could do, as I had been for months, was tell myself to only live five minutes at a time. Living one day at a time was too overwhelming for me. Too much could happen in a day, too many opportunities for intrusive thoughts that didn't belong. Five minutes gave me a better window to focus on what was important. If I could keep doing five minutes, I could get through anything.

Since it was the beginning of the year, it was a good time for reflection. During our online church service on January 3rd, our pastor spoke about reflection, and he invited elders and leaders of the church to speak. Our friend Mandy observed, "Jesus has been more present through this time than I've seen in a long time and for that, I want to stop, and I want to say thank you God." There, the pastor paused to reflect further on this, pointing out that in the middle of a desert season, Jesus has been more present and more visible to Mandy, despite this past year bringing hardship upon hardship. We were even told we could not gather as a community. Mandy then added, "It has forced us to be creative, to seek out what community and church really means to us. It has forced us to re-evaluate priorities and forge forward with showing others Christ through love and relationships in unconventional ways. We've been humbled and shown we are not in any way in control."

That comment got me thinking about it. As an example of what Mandy meant, she and her family put together a unique bag of gifts for our family during the Christmas season. They called it the twelve days of Christmas. As we were struggling with everything that was going on, Mandy and her family felt called to bless us in an unconventional way. They got twelve various small gifts and wrapped them all up with a card to go with each one. They wrapped a gift for each day, with a card to go with it explaining the significance of the gift and how it relates to Jesus. She managed to tie Jesus into a Paw Patrol colouring book, a gingerbread man pillow, socks, a bracelet, a book, and seven other things. It showed just how creative you can be with showing God's love in unconventional ways.

Back to the service, the pastor also asked the elders and leaders how our church has adapted in the last year from programming to communication. One of the key themes that Mandy and some of the elders brought up was there was a quick adaptation to the online format, and it was quite amazing to see. This, along with what Mandy had previously said, got me thinking about our current online platform and how I could be creative with seeking out community and church.

Something Jesse had gotten in the habit of recently was "checking" on us. If I was in his room playing, he would suddenly jump up and say, "I need to check on Daddy."

If we were in the kitchen and Jeremiah was on the floor in the living room, he would say, "I just need to go do something. I need to check on Jeremiah." It was so cute but also so moving. If a gesture as simple as a brother checking on his family meant so much, how else could we expand this?

I started to utilize Facebook messenger more and decided I would "check" on my friends. This has been a rough year for a lot of people. In fact, for a lot of people, relationships have been ruined, jobs have been lost, health has been depleted, and future hopes of positivity have vanished. Many have been struggling with the pandemic in numerous ways. I thought if Jesse can check on his family members, then I could check on God's family.

I started messaging friends and family to check on them. Some people I messaged were regular friends who had been there for me through this last year, some were friends from high school I hadn't seen in years, and some were community leaders who still need some encouragement as much as everybody else. By the end of January, I was averaging 50 conversations a week; it was awesome!

Originally, I started off just checking on people to see how they were doing but in my heart that just didn't feel like it was enough. I could see how desperate people were for connection, for something more. One thing that came to me from years back was a workshop I took led by a deaf person. One thing she said that stuck with me was this: In a non-deaf community, when you run into a stranger in a hallway, elevator, or line up, you politely say hello or nod your head and the conversation usually ends there. In the deaf community, when one runs into a stranger, you talk to that stranger and have a conversation until you find a connection. Eventually you will have some sort of connection, like a mutual school, friend, job, or place of residence. Once you find that connection, it is finalized, and you can part ways with that person. I just love the idea of this form of connection, so I decided to try doing that with my conversations.

Every time someone gave me a dead answer, I gave another question. I kept going and stayed persistent with each of my conversations. I just kept tossing the ball, as you say, until there was a mutual connection built. Because of this, I got to know my friends on a deeper and more intimate level. I got to know things about people that normally didn't come up in conversation. I got to help a friend out with an experience her son was going through that I had gone through as a kid. I was able to reconnect and find similarities with old friends from my childhood. It made me realize just how many people I had in my life. People were just really struggling with connection right now.

Throughout the month, my messaging had kicked off so much that I gave myself a little name. I had previously been struggling with a Netflix addiction and was always into one show or another. When I finished my last show, it was about the same time as the January 3rd church sermon. I then decided, instead of finding another show, I would message people instead. Now my "show" as I call it, is **"building connections."** I go outside with a hot cup of coffee, open my computer, and build connections. And I love it!

CHAPTER 14
FEBRUARY 2021
BITTERSWEET

Moving into February brought a new set of fears. We knew Dave would be having a PET scan soon to find out if the chemo and radiation was effective. My brain was constantly being pulled one of two ways. Would God heal him and have this all be part of our story as we share our testimony to others? Or is God's plan to put a number on Dave's last days? Would we go on to have more kids? Or would I soon be a widow taking care of our two sons alone? It was a whirlwind of emotion all the time.

We got the call that Dave would have the PET scan on the 6th and would see his oncologist via telephone appointment for results on the 11th of February. So, we would know by Valentine's Day. The days leading up to the PET scan were riddled with anxiety. Not that we would know the results on Saturday but by then the answer would be on a piece of paper somewhere. We were so anxious as was everyone else around us. I just wished there was something we could do to make extra sure the cancer was gone but there was nothing else we could do but pray.

On the Friday night before the scan, we had something beautiful happen. We were surrounded by our church in our own backyard. We had 12 people from our church come over on Friday night just to pray over Dave. It felt almost magical. Twelve people who had enough faith that prayer could heal cancer. It was freezing cold as we had an arctic air front in that week but nonetheless, they did it. Dave, shivering under a blanket, me beside him, and twelve members of our church praying over the cancer. It was beautiful!

For the next few days, the anxiety could be felt everywhere. It was in our steps as we paced through the house, it was in our voices as words were cut short, it was in the kids as they could pick it up through us, it was everywhere. In a matter of days, our lives could change forever and yet there was nothing we could do to make the time go by faster. My anxiety doesn't do well with waiting. I like to have all the answers right now. Unfortunately, God doesn't work that way.

February 11th fell on the one day of week Jesse normally does not have daycare. I tried everything to get him in, telling the daycare what was happening on the 11th but there was no guarantee they could give him a spot. We would have to wait until morning to see if anyone called in sick. That was enough anxiety on its own. Dave didn't have an appointment time for the 11th, it was just when the doctor called. We could find out by 9am or we could be waiting around the phone all day. Either way, I didn't want Jesse there picking up on all the tension. Luckily one of the other moms, who worked from home, volunteered to keep her daughter home for the day so I could secure a spot for Jesse. I accepted her offer and gracefully thanked her from the bottom of my heart. It was the biggest thing anyone could have done for me in that moment, seriously.

I had Jesse dropped off at daycare and went home to wait by the phone. By 9:30, the waiting was just impossible. I convinced Dave to call his doctor's office and ask them if they had a time for which they intended to call Dave so we wouldn't be sitting around all day waiting. Luckily, they were able to tell us they had Dave penciled in for 2pm. At least now, we had a time. I could feel the air deflate from my lungs.

Generally, when I am feeling overwhelmed, I like to go for a drive. It's the one place I feel safe to meet God and come to Him genuinely where I am at. If I need to cry, I do. If I need to scream, I can. If I need to blame and lash out and lose it a bit, then driving is that safe place for me to do that. This was a go for a drive day. Lately I had been coming up to a place called Jade Bay at Cultus Lake. It's a boat launch area but offseason it's a great place to come and just appreciate the beautiful British Columbia. It's where I have come to meet God during this whole cancer journey. It's where I take a minute to breathe and ground myself. It's where I recollect myself and gather myself together.

I got home just after one o'clock. The phone call was happening at two. Another hour until we would find out if Dave had a death sentence or a life extension. My brain kept going back and forth envisioning both different scenarios. I could see them both play out in my head, neither one more than the other. Obviously, we hoped he would be cancer free, but our faith was in God regardless of the outcome.

Finally, just after two o'clock, the phone rang. We looked at the call display and saw it was the hospital. This was it. Dave answered the phone with an eerie hello. On the other line was the oncologist, "Hello Dave, how are you today?" he said as Dave picked up. "A little anxious, in all honesty"

Dave replied, just hoping the doctor would skip to the chase. The doctor instantly responded, "Oh how come...Your PET scan came back clear." Our hearts stopped and our eyes teared up. Did we seriously just hear what we thought we heard? Dave obviously thought the same thing as he asked, "Seriously? I'm cancer free?" "Seriously" said the doctor.

I don't even remember the rest of the conversation. Dave had the phone on speakerphone, and we listened to the doctor ramble on about regular check-ups and follow up PET scans over the months and years, but our minds were elsewhere. Dave was cancer free. Who would we tell first? It felt so surreal to hear and think. Was this happening? Was Dave getting a second, or rather third, chance at life?

Last March we had received the news Dave was cancer-free. That felt real. It was a relief. It was the biggest breath of air I had felt in weeks. This time felt — not like that. I was obviously more than happy Dave was cancer free but the relief in the depth of my soul had not yet sunk in. I didn't know how long that would take, or even if it would sink in like it had before. How could it? We had heard the words, "You are cancer free" and then later heard the same doctor say, "The cancer is back". How can I relax this time knowing how possible it was for it to return?

For the next little while, I found myself needing to keep very busy. If I wasn't busy with some project or another, I was thinking; I was thinking about how and when Dave was going to die. I was thinking about how terrible it was to see him suffer like he did through treatment. I was thinking about how he was too weak to hold his own son. I was thinking about how I spent Christmas alone while he was in the hospital. All these thoughts kept intruding and weren't leaving me alone. And when they came, I broke down like a sobbing mess—every—single—time.

I couldn't seem to get past this last season. I was somewhere stuck between the terrible winter we just had, and my crippling fears the cancer was going to come back and kill him. My anxiety was at an all-time high and yet we had just gotten the best news we could ask for; Dave was cancer-free. Why couldn't I relax and sit with this wonderful news? Why did my mind have to keep going and going like the song that never ends?

One day led to the next, and nothing was getting easier. Jesse was still going to daycare, and I was really having a lot of anxiety regarding our future together. Dave was getting better and better each day though. It was a slow journey, but he felt he was ready to look at returning to work. I was so proud of him. He had gone through so much and was really bouncing back. It was truly amazing to watch despite my fears. I seemed to be the only one struggling to move on.

We were on a track slowly but surely to get back to a new normal. Dave would get back into working, Jesse was still attending daycare, Jeremiah and I spent our days at home playing peekaboo and keeping up with my email contacts. I was in my second month of my **Building Connections** ministry. It wasn't anything more than checking on friends but for so many people, it became the highlight of their week. If I didn't check on others, often they would turn around and check on me.

Over the last number of months, Dave's dad had been struggling with some health issues and was having several tests done to figure out what was going on. He and my mother-in-law had been shrugging it off for some time due to everyone's concerns with Dave over these last few months. Apparently, they were more concerned than they let on, and so were the doctors.

On February 24th, my father-in-law got the devastating news they were hoping wouldn't be true…he had ALS, amyotrophic lateral sclerosis. Despite all the research being done, ALS was something there was no cure for. He would have 2-5 years at best before it would take his life. This was such devastating news. We hadn't even had time to process this cancer journey and now Dave was facing losing his dad. We had 13 days from the time Dave was declared cancer free to the day my father-in-law was diagnosed with ALS. It didn't seem fair for our family to go through so much.

The diagnosis of my father-in-law meant many things to many people. For my mother-in-law, it meant she was losing her companion. To Dave and his siblings, it meant they were losing their dad. To Jesse, Jeremiah, and the other grandkids, they were losing their grandfather. It was heartbreaking to know what was going to happen. Jeremiah loves his Papa. In fact, I think Papa is his favourite person in the world. He was only 8 months at this time though so it was likely he would not remember Papa which was devastating. Jesse may remember but vaguely. He wouldn't get to have the memories the other grandkids got to have taking vacations with Grandma and Papa or going to the zoo or Christmas festivities.

I didn't know how we would break it to Jesse. He had been through so much already; I didn't have the heart to tell him. Dave didn't either so we decided to wait until it was closer to the time before actually explaining any of this heartbreaking news. I didn't want to put more sickness in his life just yet.

CHAPTER 15
MARCH 2021
MOVING ON

As March rolled around again, it brought the one-year anniversary of the pandemic. This March, though, the COVID-19 numbers were much higher. Starting off March 2021, Canada had seen over one million cases of COVID-19, and over 23,000 people had died. Worldwide there were 132 million cases and 2.87 million deaths. It was crazy how quickly this virus not only circulated the globe but how quickly it overwhelmed our healthcare system.

To slow down the spread of the virus, restaurants and pubs were shut down yet again, this time with only 16 hours' notice to the workers in the field. Churches and all other religious gatherings were banned and had been almost all year. There was a short window in the fall when they opened for a few weeks but were then shut down again. Masks were mandatory to wear everywhere we went. Only essential travel was allowed. It was last March all over again.

The only difference between last year and this year was life couldn't stop for us this year. Last year, we took the opportunity to stay home and potty train Jesse. We had just been out of the cancer journey (the first time), I was pregnant, and it was nice to sit and be.

This year though, there were many other things going on. Dave was preparing to go back to work, Jesse was in daycare, and life was continuing as normal only without churches, restaurants, and people to come over for coffee.

Due to my father-in-law's ALS diagnosis, we were now looking at moving. It looked like my in-laws would be selling their house at some point and since we lived in their basement suite, we needed to move. So, we began the search for a new home. Ideally, I liked the idea of a townhouse because I like the feeling of community. One local townhouse development was in the middle of being built so Dave stopped into the presentation centre one day to inquire. He grabbed an application form, and we had it filled out and dropped off the next week. Then we waited. Finally, on March 17th, we got the call we were selected! We even got to pick which unit we wanted based on a picture of the development project.

I had loved living in the basement suite of my in-laws. In fact, it was the most beautiful place I have ever lived. Our backyard overlooked the Vedder River right by the Vedder bridge. The neighbours were wonderful, I was a 15-minute walk from my dad's house, and Jesse's daycare was only a 5-minute drive. It was the perfect location. But as with many things in life, it was time to move on.

On Thursday, March 25th, I got a letter from Jesse's daycare around 4:00. It was titled "Urgent Notice." As I opened the letter and started reading, my jaw dropped. It had already been a rough day in the fact that Jesse had broken not one but two pairs of glasses in this single day, was not listening, to the point that he ran out into the parking lot and almost got hit by a car. But now there was this pressing news from his daycare. As of Monday, the 29th, the centre would be closed until further notice.

I frantically started searching online for other local daycares but over forty families were doing the same thing. I was never going to get a spot. Plus, I didn't really "need" daycare like the other families who were frantically looking for work purposes. I did need it, but I needed it for my mental health. I had been struggling but thanks to daycare, I had been able to process, journal, and even write my book! Having daycare meant Jesse had somewhere stable to go throughout the week. It meant he had structured days which was good for him as he was currently being assessed for autism.

The only daycare I could find a spot for Jesse was Kids Club, but it was all the way across town. That meant I would be driving Jesse 22 minutes out of my way and back twice a day. I thought about the necessity of daycare, but as the minutes turned into hours, my anxiety got the best of me. I needed daycare for Jesse right now. I couldn't explain it. He did so much better with the routine and the structured days, and my mental health did so much better too.

For me, my mental health is not something I talk lightly about. I have bipolar disorder, and it affects everything I do and how I do it. It affects my ability to parent, my ability to work, my ability to do everything. It is a new way of life, a way I have had to learn to adapt and do differently because of my diagnosis.

Years ago, when I first started struggling with mental health and was diagnosed bipolar, I felt lost in a completely different world. Those around me seemed to glide through life, whereas I struggled. I struggled to keep a job, I struggled to process the hard life I had been dealt from a young age, I struggled with my emotions to the point that I could not emotionally regulate without the help of medication and therapy. It brought me to a place where I was depressed, suicidal, and was a frequent flyer at the local psych ward. I felt zero purpose in this life God had given me.

Through years of counselling, medication, and my support system, I have come to a place where I can live a somewhat normal life. I have learned numerous skills and coping mechanisms to help aid me in my mental health journey, and I have become very skilled at the art of self-awareness. Being self-aware and realizing what my needs are, are essential at seeing success. Having Jesse in daycare was one of these things and luckily, my doctor agreed. Jesse switched over to Kids Club for the beginning of April and our new journey began.

CHAPTER 16
APRIL 2021
REMINISCING

We got Jesse into Kids Club across town and the drive wasn't so bad. It gave me extra time to think and pray in my day. Jesse seemed to do well with the transition into a new daycare; he ate his lunch, had a nap, and even made some new friends. One of his best friends from his old daycare had also transferred to this one so the boys got to stay together, which was neat.

One day when I picked Jesse up from daycare, I got him in the van and asked him if he wanted to go home and see Daddy. His response floored me. He said, "Daddy's in the hospital." I think I may have laughed a little because of how absurd this sounded. Dave hadn't been in the hospital since December, and we were now entering April. I told Jesse Daddy wasn't in the hospital, but he was home with Jeremiah. Jesse argued with me in his big three-year-old voice saying, "No, he isn't!". I started to get a little concerned, so I explained to Jesse that Daddy was in the hospital when he had the cancer, but the cancer is all gone now. This time, Jesse looked me right in the eye and said, "He still has his cancer a little bit." Again, I told him Daddy's cancer was all gone, but again he said, "No he has it just a little bit".

I was heartbroken. Obviously, Jesse was struggling with some big emotions from the cancer journey our family went through but I didn't realize how big. Was he struggling to get over it like I was? I had been having my own struggle trying to get over the cancer treatment. I was haunted daily by the pictures in my mind of Dave while he was sick and looking like death. Just the thought of our journey would bring tears to my eyes. I couldn't imagine how this must be for our three-year-old. I was struggling to process what I understand, how in the world could he process this?

The next morning, Dave was getting ready to go to work. He was tying up his shoes and grabbing his keys like he did every day since he started his gradual return to work. Today, Jesse looked at Daddy and asked, "Are you going to the hospital, Daddy?" Dave looked at him and reassured him that he was just going to work, and he would be home at the end of the day.

I got in touch with the child development centre that day. We already had a consultant due to his sensory disorder and his "quirks" as I called them. We had just finished filling out the forms from Sunny Hill so he would be going for an autism assessment at some point, hopefully this year. Now more than ever, I was thankful I had these supports in place. His consultant at the Child Development Centre suggested we set up a zoom meeting to figure out how to best support Jesse during this time.

After chatting with his consultant, we decided we would put a book together for Jesse to help him process all the trauma he has gone through. I needed to find photos going back to when Jesse became a big brother, Daddy was sick, when Daddy went to work, pictures of our new house we are moving to, pictures of Papa who we would lose soon, and then uplifting positive photos to fill him up with the happy memories. I needed to find photos of Jesse with his friends, Jesse wearing matching clothes with his brother, Jesse having snuggles and tickles with Daddy, and Jesse smiling in as many happy and "normal" photos as I could find. Putting this book together was so hard on my heart. It was a physical reminder of all our trauma of the last year.

It was hard to see a physical reminder of the trauma my child was subjected to at three years old. When I had a baby in 2017, I never expected to put a book together of his "trauma" at three years old. But as hard as it was, I had to keep reminding myself this was part of God's plan. Nothing happens by mistake. God has a good plan for all His children, even if it is a plan, we ourselves do not understand.

Each day we watched the health of my father-in-law decline as we watched Dave's health improve. It was like watching the life flow from one body to another. Day by day, Dave was getting better as his dad was getting worse. Dave was gradually returning to work as his dad closed accounts for the people he did work for. Dave was slowly gaining back the strength to do all the things he did before cancer, while his dad lost the ability to do so many things, he recently did without concern.

Dave's physical health was drastically improving. He still didn't have saliva which was a constant struggle for him, and he still got tired very easily, but overall, he was back to his normal self. By this point, he had even taken Jeremiah to the grocery store for groceries on his own. He had taken Jesse out on his bike, brought up the garbage can on garbage day, and was about to have his first five-day work week. It was incredible to watch!

Dave's mental health, on the other hand, was starting to decline. This had been such a hard time for our family, and we had no time to process, before moving on to the next thing. Dave had a PTSD diagnosis from 2017. He was dispatching for the police department and took on too many tough calls that affected his mind and his ability to perform his job and home life. His mental health in 2017 was one of the toughest things we had walked through in our marriage (at that point). Dave worked so hard through therapy, counselling, and his own determination to overcome his PTSD. Now it looked like it might be returning.

Here I was struggling myself, carrying my confused three-year-old and my struggling husband. There was no way I could do it on my own. Who could? Luckily, I didn't have to. I have God on my side who promises to carry us when we can no longer carry ourselves. We only must ask. It's so hard to ask though. I really detest having to ask for help. If there is any chance at all that I can do something myself, I will not ask for help. This was a time, however, where I needed God's help, strength, provision, and support. I needed help, and I needed someone to carry me through this very difficult time.

CHAPTER 17
MAY 2021
SPEECHLESS

As the month of May started off, the air was filled with all the unknowns. We didn't know if Jesse's old daycare would open again. We didn't know what day we could move into our new house. And we didn't know how much longer we had with my father-in-law. His disease was progressing so quickly taking away his ability to even talk. By the end of the month, he was able to slur a few words but was minimally understood. How could this have progressed so quickly?

Dave was doing his gradual return to work still but was working mainly from home at this point because of the new COVID-19 variant going around. Apparently, the Delta variant was more deadly than the original COVID-19 virus, so workplaces were being asked to move staff home if possible. In Dave's case, because of his recent cancer treatment, his work was very quick to accommodate him at home.

I spent most of the month packing everything and preparing Jesse for the move. Every day after daycare, we would drive over to the new house first and go ride his bike around the neighbourhood. I wanted him to get used to going straight there after daycare, and I wanted him to familiarize himself with the new house as much as possible. Jesse didn't do well with change, so we had to do our best to meet him in the middle and help that change be less shocking.

Jesse and Mommy selfie out front of our new house being built

Come moving day (days), we had some help! The COVID-19 vaccines were being rolled out finally and the numbers were starting to go down. This meant people were more willing to step out of their bubble, and come help us. My dad and some other friends volunteered to come on the Friday and help move all our boxes to the new house in their vehicles, which was a huge help. On Saturday I had some friends from our church come over and help me unpack and set up everything. Two people were upstairs putting together Jesse's new IKEA bed and some other furniture, and two others unpacked my entire kitchen for me!

On Saturday night, when Jesse came home, it was exactly that. It was home. He was so excited to come up the stairs and go looking for his new room. He was excited to see the new bed set up he had picked from IKEA. He was absolutely thrilled to show it off to his friend Madelyn when Christina brought him home. That made my heart so happy. To see him so excited and happy in his new environment brought me so much joy.

As we sat around the TV at the end of the day watching a hockey game (because we had to test the tv and of course, you must test it with hockey, duh!), Dave got a call from his older brother. I couldn't hear what was being said, but Dave's reaction showed it wasn't good. It was utter shock and horror from what he was hearing. After he got off the phone, he looked at me and explained what had happened.

Just an hour after we moved out, his dad took a bad fall in the garage. My mother-in-law called an ambulance who took him to the hospital where he had stitches and a CT scan. Luckily, he was well enough to return home, but precautions had to be put in place. He was no longer well enough to be left unattended and that was a hard reality.

CHAPTER 18

JUNE 2021

FATHER'S DAY

Over the following days, Dave and his siblings had repeated conversations on how they could best work together and make sure someone was always there. Dave planned with his work to work from home every Monday but work at his parents. That way, his mom could make plans on Mondays to go to the grocery store or take care of other appointments. As of June 1st, Dave's work did have everybody back working in the office, but they were happy to accommodate him in this way.

Dave's sister was planning on coming over from the coast every Tuesday and spend the night. She wanted to make sure her mom had at least one night a week where there was help there if needed. Between the other siblings and various visitors coming and going, they were pretty set.

Shortly after we moved, Dave wanted to have my in-laws over to show them our new place. My father-in-law hadn't been doing too well since the fall, so we thought it was best to have this visit quickly. Jesse was so excited to have Grandma and Papa come to our new house. Unfortunately, though, it was a whole flight of stairs just to get to our main living space and another flight to get to the bedrooms.

Papa couldn't make it all the way to Jesse's room, but he was able to make it to our main living area and sit at the kitchen table.

Jesse wanted to give Grandma the grand tour of the whole house, so while the kids and I took her upstairs to show her around, Dave and his dad had a little talk in the kitchen. It was nice except it wasn't a talk. It was Dave talking and his dad writing questions and answers down on a piece of paper. My father-in-law was 100% nonverbal now. I can't imagine how that must feel to have your voice swept away from you. He still did such an awesome job smiling though and keeping the room alive despite all that was happening to him. It was inspiring for sure.

The next week when Dave went to work, I took that piece of paper with all his dad's writing, and I laminated it. I wanted to save it for Dave for Father's Day. I wanted him to have something special to remember his dad by. He can no longer cherish the vocal conversations, but this is still a conversation with his dad, nonetheless.

By the time Father's Day rolled around, COVID-19 restrictions were finally starting to lift. Nonessential travel was allowed throughout our province, gatherings of up to 50 people were allowed outdoors and up to six people were allowed inside. Vaccinations were rolling out, and by this time 75% of Canadians had their first dose already. This meant that finally, after 16 long months, families could start to gather again and what good timing too.

It was perfect timing for the restrictions to lift. Dave, as well as his other siblings, needed to see their dad for Father's Day. This was likely going to be his last Father's Day; the family needed to be together. We decided to plan an outdoor event at my sister-in-law's house. It was a beautiful celebration and so nice to have everybody together again.

Dave and his dad on Father's Day

A week after Father's Day, my father-in-law was getting weaker and even he wondered if he would see his 75th birthday in just a couple of short months. A couple of nurses from palliative home care came by to see him and offer their services that week. They asked my father-in-law how long he thought he had. His answer was two to three months. He was feeling so weak and physically unwell, he figured two or three months was all he had left.

It was heartbreaking to think he could feel the time of his pending death. We were all hurting while also shocked to think about how fast this had happened. It was only the beginning of summer and yet we were already mourning the loss of our dear Father and Grandfather. This was just what was happening in our world. The rest of our province was dealing with the dramatic blow of a rare but deadly heat dome that covered most of the provincial area.

Approaching the heat wave at the end of June, scientists warned it would shatter the all-time temperature records throughout the province and it did. The temperature recorded for highest on record was in Lytton, which was 49.5 Celsius (121.1 Fahrenheit)! The highest we reached in Chilliwack was 44C (111.2F), and it was hot! It was so hot; you couldn't stand outside for more than a few minutes without burning. The sun touching your skin made it ache, it was so hot. I think the worst part was how it never cooled off in between each day. Nighttime lows were still in the high 30's. Nothing got a chance to cool down after overheating. The heat was literally trapped everywhere in our province with nowhere to go, it was terrible. Laying there at night even with air-conditioning, our skin would drop beads of sweat onto the already soaking bed sheet. We all just prayed the heat dome would subside and we could all go back to normal.

After the heat dome hovered over British Columbia for a few days, it began to move eastward. It sparked 100's of fires throughout the province which were rapidly spreading from town to town. Multiple towns around BC were put on evacuation alerts and orders, due to the proximity of the fires. It was getting scary.

CHAPTER 19

JULY 2021

PREPARING FOR GOODBYE

By the middle of July, more than 3000 square km of land had been burned by over 1000 different fires in the province. On July 20th, the Public Safety Minister declared a state of emergency. The White Rock Lake fire in the Thompson Nicola District was the worst one yet. It started July 13th, and by the end of July, the fire covered 30,000 hectares between Kamloops and Vernon. It continued to burn until it covered 833 square kilometres by mid-September. Even though we were finally over the heat dome, the province continued to burn.

My father-in-law's care was getting to be too much at home, so the family was now looking at private home care. While the search was on for setting up private home care, Dave and his siblings took turns spending the night at the house to care for their dad through the night. My father-in-law wore a call alert necklace around his neck. It would ring a buzzer in the spare room. Whoever was staying, would then get up to assist Dad with whatever he needed.

One day the perfect opportunity came to talk to Jesse about his Papa. At this time in Jesse's life, he was very interested in road names and what roads lead to where. One morning on the way to Walmart, he randomly asked me where the road is that goes to Heaven. I figured this was the opportune moment and I should take it. I explained to him there isn't a road to Heaven because it's not a place you go to until you are all done living here on Earth. When we are all done, then we die, and God calls us to Heaven. I explained to him this happens when people get older, like Grandma and Papa. I couldn't yet tell him Papa was going to Heaven, but I knew I would need to soon.

Dave and his siblings had been working on a special project for my father-in-law for his birthday. They got a short video clip sent in from friends and family members wishing my father-in-law a happy birthday and telling him how much they love him. Kim put it all together into a video to give to my father-in-law on his birthday. Seeing how quickly he was deteriorating, the family didn't want to wait. His actual birthday wasn't until the end of August, but we weren't sure where his health would be at that time, so we did it in July.

The party went beautifully. We were all together as a family to celebrate this wonderful soul turning 75! When it was time to play the video, we all gathered in the living room. There, for the first time, Dave saw his dad cry. It was the sweetest, most heartfelt moment, and one we would all cherish forever. We were so thankful the COVID-19 restrictions were starting to ease, and we were able to have this party together. It meant so much to everyone, especially my father-in-law.

It was a good thing we did the birthday party for my father-in-law earlier in the month because over the next few weeks, he continued to decline faster and faster. By the end of July, he could no longer be cared for at home and was sent to palliative care. At this point, we didn't know how much longer we had with him, but we knew it wouldn't be long.

CHAPTER 20
AUGUST 2021
MOURNING

The family were all taking turns rotating who was going to stay with my father-in-law. We didn't want him to be alone, ever. I took Jeremiah on the holiday Monday while Jesse went to visit a friend. There, we said our goodbyes. I brought Jeremiah over to his Papa to give him one more hug, but he pulled back. This wasn't typical of Jeremiah; Papa was his favourite person in the world. We thought maybe Jeremiah didn't recognize him in this element though. Papa couldn't hold him, couldn't talk, couldn't even lift his head, or breathe independently. It must have been scary for a little guy who couldn't understand any of it.

We didn't stay at the hospital long because we didn't want to overwhelm my father-in-law too much. When we got back to Chilliwack to pick Jesse up, I saw Jeremiah was not quite himself. He was very lethargic and starting to burn up. When he saw Jesse and still clung on to me, I knew something was wrong. He was getting hotter and hotter every minute. I had to ask my friend for Tylenol because I didn't typically carry it around with me, not with my second born anyway!

That night, we dosed with Tylenol and Advil around the

clock and milk, milk, milk. I was just working on weaning, so I didn't have a lot of milk, but the breast was the only thing my little guy wanted. It was so sad to see him like that. It was hard to keep his fever down too. At one point, he went up to 103.1! By morning, I knew he needed medical attention.

We went to emergency first thing the next morning. They took us in quick, probably because of his raging fever. After answering question after question, the doctor asked if he could do a chest X-ray. The way to do a chest X-ray on a baby is to put them in this little tube contraption that holds their arms up in the air and keeps them perfectly still. In this little tube, Jeremiah cried and cried and cried. I wished I could stand right beside him and hold his little hands sticking out the top of that tube, but I wasn't allowed. Because of the radiation from the X-ray, I had to walk away and stand in the bathroom, leaving my baby all alone. It was terrible.

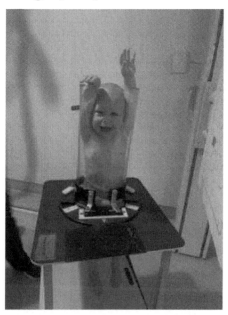

Jeremiah preparing for a chest X-ray

Luckily it only took a couple of minutes and then Jeremiah was free to come out and back into my arms. We were brought back to our bed in emergency, where we waited for the doctor to view the results and come back. It didn't take long for the doctor to return. He told me Jeremiah had "viral pneumonia," and there was nothing they could do but to rotate the Tylenol and Advil until the fever was gone. They said if he didn't start to improve in a couple of days, to come back in.

Unfortunately for Jeremiah, we were still in the pandemic and since he came in with a fever, he had to have a covid test. The covid tests were terrible. You had to lean your head back while a doctor gets a swab from up your nose way at the back. Not only does this feel incredibly uncomfortable, but the doctor then needs to keep the stick up the nose and rotate it around for five whole seconds. It was terrible watching my baby being put through that.

A chest X-ray, a covid test, and four hours later, we were done and were free to go home and rotate Tylenol and Advil some more. It was viral and it needed to run its course. I was thankful it wasn't anything more serious.

The next couple of days were terrible. Jeremiah slept and burnt up all day. He still wouldn't eat, couldn't be put down, was extremely lethargic, and my momma heart was really starting to worry. I brought Jesse to daycare the next morning and we went back to emergency. I just felt in my gut five days was too long to be fighting a fever and this didn't seem normal to me. He also wasn't peeing nearly enough, so I was starting to worry about potential dehydration.

Luckily, we didn't have to wait long before a nurse was

calling out Jeremiah's name. His vitals were taken, and a doctor was on the way already, wow! Once the doctor came, he asked me a series of questions about Jeremiah's health and current symptoms. I explained that I felt this was going on for too long and it didn't feel right to me. I felt in my gut that something was wrong. Instantly the doctor shut his clipboard and said, "Done, I'll bring in a paediatrician." I was so relieved. I felt validated! I just wanted my little guy to get better, he was only 13 months old, after all.

While we waited for the paediatrician, a few other tests had to be run on my sick baby. They wanted to repeat the chest X-ray and do some bloodwork. I anticipated the bloodwork would be a lot of screaming but miraculously it wasn't. The hospital used these little numbing pads that stuck to his skin for a few minutes before the blood was drawn. He was so lethargic anyway; he barely noticed the needle go in.

A couple hours later, they moved us up to paediatrics. It was so much nicer in paediatrics, and quieter! It was an amazing experience being up in an area that specializes with kids, an area without beeping, loud people, and bright lights everywhere. It was almost peaceful in a weird sort of way.

The paediatrician came in quickly and went over Jeremiah's symptoms. The biggest concern at hand was his dehydration. He was only peeing about twice a day and not consuming anything other than breast milk. This sudden demand did not miraculously increase my milk supply, so I did not have as much fluid as my sick little man needed. The doctor decided an IV would be the best and most effective treatment for him, and it might even perk him up.

Once the IV was in and Jeremiah was settled for a nap,

the doctor came back in to talk to me. He pulled up a chair and sat beside the bed. I was starting to get nervous. Was this a normal thing in paediatrics because I'm just used to a doctor hovering over you prescribing antibiotics and sending you on your way. The doctor wanted to talk to me about Jeremiah's bloodwork.

There were some concerning red flags in his bloodwork. His white blood cell count was flagged low, his red blood cell count was flagged low, and his platelet count was flagged low. Apparently if all three of these are flagged low, it can be a cause for concern. The doctor continued talking but all I heard was "bone marrow…". It can be a sign of a bone marrow cancer. I checked out instantly. He kept talking, and I exited into dreamland. I couldn't deal with hearing that word again and so soon, especially when it came to my baby.

At some point, the conversation was over, and the doctor exited the room, but I honestly can't tell you what he said to me after I heard that "C" word. My focus at this point was getting my boy hydrated again and start seeing some improvement. Watching him sleep while the IV replenished his fluids was peaceful but scary at the same time. It's always peaceful to watch a baby sleep but seeing them hooked up to anything can be scary, especially for the first time. And that was before thinking about the "C" word.

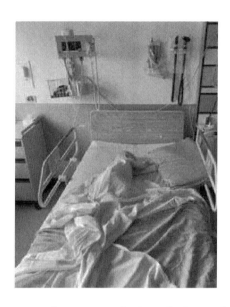

Jeremiah getting IV fluids in the hospital

Over the last week, my father-in-law was doing worse and worse. It was sad to watch. I couldn't imagine having all your bodily functions stripped away from you while still being completely coherent. My father-in-law was left unable to talk, smile, lift his head, even breathe. He was at a point in his ALS journey, where he was so uncomfortable all the time and in constant pain but still 100% present in his mind. I just couldn't imagine the strength it takes to endure that kind of suffering.

I wished I could be more support to Dave during this time, but I was spending every day in the hospital with Jeremiah. I felt so bad for Dave who had to worry about his dying Dad in one hospital and his sick son in another hospital. He knew and trusted I had Jeremiah's needs covered and taken care of though. I just wished I could meet more of Dave's needs. He was losing his dad and I was solely focused on Jeremiah. And what about Jesse? He was having so many issues at daycare and home. I just wished so bad I could help my whole family feel better from all of it.

By the time a week had gone by since Jeremiah's fever spiked, he was finally discharged from the hospital and was able to have the IV taken out of his arm. It was a marvellous day. We were still worried about the concerning bloodwork, but we would know more in a week or two. In the meantime, he appeared healthy, happy, and back to his normal smiley self.

My father-in-law was not doing so well. It was evident he was at the end; it was too hard for his body to keep working to stay alive. The family all agreed to have a doctor remove the bi-pap machine the next day and let nature run its course. It was probably the hardest decision ever made by the family, but it wasn't fair to keep him alive and suffering for everyone else's sake.

Waking up on the morning of August 9th was tense. I got out of bed at 4:30 am; I knew it was going to be a high anxiety, and highly emotional day. The family would all be waking up shortly, preparing themselves to say goodbye to our dear Dad/Papa/Grandpa. It was a hard thing to come to terms with. I chose not to tell Jesse about the day because I didn't want him to be thinking about it all day at daycare. I would tell him later.

I dropped him off at daycare and headed out to Abbotsford. Dave didn't want me to go to the hospital yet because it was only his mom and siblings currently there. He didn't want me to go far though, because he wanted me to be able to come back at any time if it was the time. It brought me back to the days where I dropped him off out front the doors to the cancer centre. My first thought was to go to community services. I needed to pick up a certificate anyway and I hadn't seen Liz and Cindy in a long time.

Sitting in the family centre room brought me back. How I wished groups were up and running at this point, but they were still shut down from the restrictions. Things had just started opening but now they were talking about a fourth wave. I think everyone and their dog at this point were exhausted from COVID-19. Nonetheless, it was nice to sit in the family centre room, have somewhere for Jeremiah to crawl around, enjoy some great company, and I was close enough by, I could get to the hospital in ten minutes if Dave called.

After a while, it was clear Jeremiah needed a nap desperately. There was no way I would want to bring him into the hospital with him being as whiny as he was being. I decided to buckle him up in his car seat, turn on the radio, and hit the freeway. We headed Westbound on the number one highway until he fell asleep, and then we turned around to head back. I couldn't be too far away from the hospital in case I got the call. It was a good thing I turned around when I did because not too long later, Dave called me. It was almost time to take the bi-pap machine out, but the family was taking some time to go outside and take a few deep breaths first.

By this point, I was back close to the hospital, so I drove straight there, even if it was just to hug my husband. They were only allowing immediate family in now so I couldn't go inside anyway. But I was here to hug him. One thing about Dave is he gives the biggest most amazing hugs. Mine are nothing in comparison but I tried with all my might, I really did! After a brief visit and an amazing hug, it was time. It was time for Dave and his siblings to go back in and say goodbye to their dad one last time.

Jeremiah had woken up and appeared hungry, so I took him to McDonald's for a chicken nugget happy meal. Apparently, he was hungry because he ate three whole nuggets himself and half his fries. Usually, he nibbles on one piece of nugget, plays with a couple, and throws the fries all over the floor. This was truly a McDonald's milestone! When he was done, I figured we should get back in the van and be prepared for the call.

Jeremiah and Mommy McDonald's selfie

Just after I buckled Jeremiah up in his car seat and turned the van on, I got a call from Dave. "Dad's gone." was the first thing I heard from the other end when I picked up the phone. It happened so fast, I barely made it a couple blocks away for something to eat. I was so thankful I stayed this close. I headed back to the hospital to give Dave the ultimate, biggest, deepest hug from the very depth of my soul. It still didn't beat his hugs, but I had to give it my best.

Embracing Dave as he held on to me crying was so beautiful. All his might came out in that hug, and I could tell just how much he needed this. I was so thankful I stayed close. I wished I could have sat with him hugging in the parking lot for the next two hours. It had been such a rough year already; we just weren't ready for this. But Dave had to go in and start working on the call list his family had put together. It was broken up into five groups, one for each sibling. Dave comes from a large Dutch family, so it was quite a long list!

After everyone had been called, my mother-in-law and the five kids were ready to leave the hospital. Everyone was gathering at my in-law's house for dinner. We just needed to be together. I headed back to Chilliwack and braced myself to give Jesse this hard news. I didn't even know how to tell him. We had been talking to him for some time about Heaven and how when it's your turn to die, Jesus will bring you to live with Him in Heaven. Then we introduced that Papa was sick and was going to go to Heaven soon. Now it was time to tell him the final part of the chapter.

I got to Jesse's daycare with such a heavy heart. In a weird way, I didn't want to go in and pick him up because I knew I was going to break his little heart and I just didn't want to do that to him. He had never experienced death before, not even an animal, so this was all new to him. I walked into the daycare bracing myself for what I had to do. I rang the buzzer at the front of the door and waited while my heart rate skyrocketed somewhere into space. I saw Jesse running my way yelling, "Mommy!" with such a happy smile on his face, a smile I was surely going to turn upside down. I didn't want to do this to him.

As we got in the car, I told him I wanted to talk to him about something important. It was as if he knew; he said, "Is it Papa?" I told him yes, it was his Papa. Next Jesse asked, "Did Papa go to Heaven?" I was proud he had retained this information, but it was so hard hearing the words come from the mouth of a three-year-old boy. I explained to him Papa got too sick and it was time for his body to die because it wasn't working very well. I told Jesse Papa was all better now he was in Heaven with Jesus. Jesse looked at me and asked, "Can Papa talk now?" A smile grew across my face because he seemed to understand what I was saying, and he was asking all the questions. "Yes Honey, Papa can talk now. He's all better and he gets to live with Jesus now."

Jesse seemed content with that conversation, so I thought it was probably best to leave it at that and let him absorb that information for a while and give him time to process everything. I guess he was still processing because the next thing he said was, "Tomorrow when I die, I am going to see Papa and talk to him in Heaven." Oh, why was this so hard? I looked at him and explained he isn't going to die for a long, long time and he didn't need to worry about it now. I can't imagine how confusing death must be for such a young child. I wished I could jump into his brain and see where all the wires were crossed and fix them all up so he could understand.

As we got to my in-law's house, we could see it was full of people. Everyone was stopping by to offer their condolences. Dave already had Jeremiah, so it was just Jesse and I who walked into the house. It felt different. Knowing the whole family was here but my father-in-law wasn't, was weird. Knowing we would never see him sitting in his chair again was hard. Seeing my mother-in-law with sunken eyes at the harsh reality of losing her husband to a terrible disease that day was devastating.

Over the next few days, we did what we could to recover. We were recovering from losing my father-in-law and we were also recovering from Jeremiah being so sick. Now it was time to be home and rest. The funeral was set for the next Tuesday, so Dave took a second week off work. His presence was also a comfort as I worked at helping Jeremiah get better.

The weekend passed in a blur and Monday was here before we knew it. Monday evening was the viewing of my father-in-law. I was not raised with this tradition, so it was all new to me. The evening before the funeral, the family, and friends of the deceased gather around the body at the funeral home to say one last goodbye. I had done this with Dave once before, but it was as a supportive spouse who didn't really know the deceased. This time, it was my father-in-law, and I really wasn't sure how I felt about it. All I could picture was him smiling or telling me "Oh it's only 5 minutes" every time I thanked him for picking up Jesse from daycare. I couldn't let go of the memory of him walking down the outside stairs to come and grab my garbage can in the middle of winter when Dave was in the hospital. He was 74 years old but still more concerned about me being alone with two young kids that he took care of getting my garbage can up... every week. And now I was about to go say goodbye to his dead body lying in a casket.

I pulled into the parking lot of Woodlawn's Funeral home in Abbotsford about ten minutes early. Dave was already there. I could feel myself starting to tense and shake. I got out the car and slowly walked inside with Dave by my side. There is nothing joyful about walking into a funeral home. You don't even pretend to smile when you're there.

By a few minutes after six, all the family were there and inside the waiting room. All my nieces and nephews were there, which was amazing. I was so proud of them. They were significantly older than Jesse though. They range from 11-16 so they were far more mentally mature to handle a situation like this.

Sitting there in the waiting room, no one really knew what was going to happen or how this was all going to play out. Were we all walking into the room together? Would it be one person at a time? No one knew. Finally, the funeral home employee came in the waiting room and explained how this would go. First, my mother-in-law and her five children were going to go in first for as long as they needed to. When they felt ready, the "kids" would come out and find their spouse and go back in. We did do one couple at a time at that point out of respect for privacy. It's a hard moment to say goodbye to someone you love so much.

A few minutes later, Dave and his siblings came walking out of the room. Mom stayed there by Dad's side. I wouldn't be able to leave Dave's side if that were him. Just six months ago, this was a very real possibility for Dave. I braced myself to walk in there. I told myself to stay strong, but I gave myself permission to fall apart if I needed to. I had grace on myself either way. I think that is so important during the hard times. I held Dave's hand and prepared for this walk to the front. The room almost looked like a small chapel. The casket was at the front with a picture of my Father-in-law beside it. The chapel had about ten rows of seating. We walked to the front of the chapel.

We spent a few minutes at the front with my father-in-law. Seeing him lay there was just so shocking. I don't know what I was expecting. I don't know if I expected him to look like he did a few months ago when we had family photos. I don't know if I had expected him to move. I was just in shock. I just stood quietly, staring at his body lying in a coffin at the front of a room set up for a funeral. Dave moved first by reaching his hand out and holding Dad's hand. He looked at me with his eyes full of tears saying, "I held this hand when he took his last breath". I just hugged Dave tight and rubbed his back wishing I could make his pain go away.

Eventually, it was time for us to walk away. The other siblings and spouses wanted to come spend some time with Dad too before the extended family and friends came at 7:00. Walking away from him was harder than walking towards him. Now I knew what to expect and I would do it all over again. It didn't seem right he was gone; it couldn't be.

Between Jeremiah being in the hospital and my father-in-law dying, my body snapped back into hypomania. I was quite thankful because I was getting to be in a bit of a depression, and that would not help things right now. When I am in a depression, I can't think straight, I can't respond, I can't carry a conversation, I honest to God feel like I can't even mom and that's a scary thought if my kids ever heard me say it. Hypomania, although part of my bipolar diagnosis, is not always a bad thing for me. I will often need less sleep, have more energy, and can accomplish more tasks in less time. It's generally how my body chooses to cope in tough situations. Left untreated though, it can result in full mania which can leave one hospitalized until treated adequately.

Going to bed Monday night was tough. We were mentally exhausted and knew the next day would be even more tiring. A funeral was tough at the best of times. I don't know if either Dave or I got a lot of sleep that night. Suddenly it was morning and time to get up. I don't even know if we slept. The funeral wasn't until one o'clock, so we had some time to get ourselves oriented with the idea that we were having a funeral for my father-in-law today.

We weren't sure if we were going to bring Jesse to the funeral or not. I decided to seek some counsel from someone at the Chilliwack Hospice Society. My gut was leaning towards not bringing him because we didn't want to scar him anymore than necessary. Dave was on board with that and agreed. However, upon talking with someone at the Chilliwack Hospice Society, she explained to me children who attend the funeral service generally do better with healing because they have more of an opportunity to process everything. If you don't keep talking about the situation and normalizing it, it can turn into a trauma for a child. She thought it was in the best interest of Jesse to attend the funeral even though he was only three years old.

So, Tuesday morning began with very heavy hearts. We knew there would be nothing joyful today about saying goodbye to a wonderfully beautiful soul. We knew he was in a better place now, but it was still so hard to say that final goodbye. Preparing to say goodbye to someone you love so much, there's just nothing you can do to prepare for that. There are no black clothes suitable enough, no shoes perfect enough, no hairstyle just right to say goodbye. It's something you want to present yourself for but there is just no right way.

Dave's cousin was flying in from out of town for the funeral. Dave had offered to pick her up in Vancouver at 7:30 am because he has the kindest soul of anyone I have ever met. He would go to the end of the world and back for anyone, especially family. His cousin hung out with us for the morning while we prepared for this very depressing day. It was nice to have her here to get another woman's opinion on my outfit and shoes. There just wasn't anything that felt right. She had a good time with Jesse and Jeremiah, and it was good to catch up with family despite the circumstances.

When it was time to leave, Dave and his cousin went in one vehicle and the boys, and I went in another. There was no way I was bringing Jeremiah to the funeral because he was currently a non-walking one-year-old who wanted to scream to go down and crawl all over everywhere. I can't think of anything more stressful; that was not happening. My friend Christina watched Jeremiah for me, so we dropped him off there on the way to the funeral. At the church, we dressed Jesse up in his black dress shirt and tie, he was so handsome. I was proud to have him there, being a part of this but also worried about him too. This was a lot to process.

We got to the church shortly after 12:30 pm. We had a half-hour to gather and walk in as a family. We all met in the fellowship hall where we would later have coffee and cookies. It was bittersweet being back in that church. It was sad obviously to be there today, but this was the church where Dave and I were married, so there were some good memories too, memories we would gladly cherish forever.

Before we knew it, it was one o'clock and the pastor was gathering the family, instructing us what to do. Mom would go in first with the two daughters by her side and the rest of the kids, spouses, and grandkids would follow behind. The rest of the attendees were already sitting in their pews, but they stood up at our entrance. We walked right to the front and gathered in the front three pews. The church was packed with people who loved my father-in-law very much. Later we found out the parking lot was so full, they had to direct some people to park in the parking lot next door. They intended to fill every second pew because of COVID-19 safety measures, but we were shoulder-to-shoulder in every pew. That goes to show what a man my father-in-law was. Not only were the church and parking lot full, but online there were hundreds of people from all over the world watching the service. He made that much of an impact on the world around him.

The funeral began with a welcoming prayer and psalter 245. A psalter is an old hymn sung in many churches, especially those with older generations. It was nice to be reminded through music of where my father-in-law was now, safely in the arms of Jesus, pain free. There was a beautiful sermon spoken by the pastor of the church. The pastor and his family have been friends with Dave's family for years. They lost their fifteen-year-old daughter to a tragic ski accident back in 2017 so they understand death on a very personal and intimate level.

Following the sermon, Dave and his four siblings spoke beautiful eulogies. Everything they said was so eloquently put, and it all tied together perfectly. My father-in-law would be proud to hear the way his children spoke of him. He was a man to look up to, a man who set a great example of love and kindness, and a man who dedicated his life to God, his family, and his church. He was a man who would be dearly missed by those around him.

After the funeral at the church was over, the family filed out one row at a time and began our way to our vehicles, where we would follow the hearse to the graveside for a special graveside service. I think the hardest part about this was explaining it to Jesse. I had spent so long explaining to him when people die, they go to heaven. Now he was about to see his Papa's casket get buried in the ground. I prayed God would help me direct him one step at a time and only give him the information he needed to process what he could process at this time.

As we followed the hearse down Mt Lehman road, my heart was pounding. Currently, I was in Dave's car with him and his cousin. I was crammed in the back in between two car seats explaining to Jesse what was about to happen while maintaining composure for Dave. Why did my three-year-old have so many questions?! Like seriously, so many! I introduced the word "soul" to him and tried my best to explain how our soul goes to heaven but yes, our bodies go into the ground. It was such a difficult concept to explain to a preschooler who desperately wanted to understand everything there was to know about everything.

We parked the car, and Jesse immediately asked, "Where is Papa's body?" I explained that it was in the hearse at the front of the line-up of cars, but he had to walk up and see it for himself. I walked him up with Dave by my side and we stood back and looked at the hearse. Before we knew it, it was time for the graveside memorial to begin. Jesse and I stepped back while Dave, his brothers, uncle, and nephew, pulled my father-in-law out from the hearse and carried his body to its destination at the end of the graveyard.

Jesse didn't seem to understand in too much detail quite what was happening. He asked why the flowers were there from the church. He asked why everybody was standing. He asked when it was time to go. It must have been hard for a three-year-old to be so patient for so long, but he was doing well, and I was so proud of him! When it was time to say goodbye, we encouraged Jesse to take a flower and place it on Papa's casket and he did. I don't know if he fully understood the representation, but he will one day, and I am so thankful we have that memory.

It was hard to see so many people mourn at one time, so many smiles upside down, so many tears being poured over a man who we would never get to see again. His life on earth was over. My mother-in-law was now without a husband, my husband and his siblings without a father, Jesse and seven other grandkids without having their papa and grandpa at their side again. This was devastating. I don't know if I've ever had someone this close to me pass away. All I wanted was to get walking back to the car before the tears came streaming down my face. I was ready to break, and I just didn't want to do it here. I know it was the perfect time, but I'm funny like that, it'll be the most random moment I break down.

After the graveside memorial, we all went back to the church for some coffee and snacks. I stood in the food line up to get a plate of cookies for Jesse, but I wasn't hungry. There was just nothing there that appealed to me other than a cup of warm coffee. Jesse was not wanting anything here either and was starting to get whiney and tired. It was clear he was emotionally done. I decided to leave the church early and go to Christina's where Jeremiah and Jesse's good friend Madelyn was. We had plans with the family in a couple of hours and I figured this would be a good and pleasant distraction for him.

Jesse and Madelyn played for an hour; Jeremiah had milk, and Christina and I had a good catch-up visit. It was nice to be able to get away for a bit but there was some guilt associated with it. I felt bad for not being right by Dave's side through all this. I left him all alone to give Jesse a break. I just prayed he was relying on God's strength to get him through this time until we could be together again at my sister-in-law's later that evening.

Eventually, Dave texted me telling me everyone was at my sister-in-law's house, and they had rented a food truck! I grabbed the kids, headed across town, and yes, there was a food truck parked in the driveway. Dave's sister and her husband own a greenhouse, so they have tons of property. It was the perfect place to set up a food truck and get together with family. I'm not sure who set it up, but it was brilliant. Dave was in his glory when he realized it was a Dutch food truck. He lives for Dutch food, and we just don't make it enough at home.

We stayed for a couple of hours, appreciating the time to be together with extended family. Everyone was so supportive and showed an enormous amount of compassion and love. I just love that about Dave's family.

They are all such big-hearted people. By eight o'clock though, it was clear how done and overtired the kids were. They were dragged out all day and put out of their element. Now it was past their bedtime and there was no denying it. Luckily, we had the two vehicles there, so I was free to go home and put the boys to sleep while Dave stayed with his family.

When I came home, I was overwhelmed with emotion. I felt like I couldn't do it. The fact it was after nine now and both boys were overtired was one thing, but they had both been playing in the dirt piles there and were absolutely covered from head to toe. They needed a bath before bed, or they were probably going to itch like crazy tonight. Around the time I got home, my friend Gina messaged to see how I was doing. I told her the truth; I was about to fall apart. She was at my door in fifteen minutes here to help me with the kids. She got the kids bathed while I got all their bedtime stuff ready and the rooms cleaned up, then she hung around for a bit and chatted over tea and what a day it had been.

Dave didn't leave until ten. It was a long day, but I think the family didn't want to say goodbye. It was nice to have some cheerful family time since everyone had such heavy hearts. If you put enough Dutch people together with a food truck, a good time will be had, and it was. Dave felt terrible for staying so late, but we knew he needed to stay with his family. I was covered at home thanks to Gina and now that Dave was home, we could try to unwind and settle from this emotionally hectic day.

Dave still had the rest of the week booked off. I thought about keeping Jesse home from daycare, but he wanted to go play with his friends. Dave and I felt the distraction would probably be good for him anyway. I let the daycare know to call me if he was having a rough day, and I would come grab him at any time. He said goodbye and skipped off to find his friends like a regular day. He was so happy to be here playing with his friends. Perhaps he was really feeling the urge to have some "normal".

Dave didn't feel like doing a whole lot that day. He needed to process everything now that it was all said and done. He does his best processing when he can check out on his devices, so I left him to that. I had recently shown interest in bike riding, so I spent various parts of the day processing at slightly faster speeds. There was nothing quite like feeling the wind blow through my hair, even with my helmet on. To feel the breeze brush up against my face as I sped down the road was exhilarating. There just wasn't anything that compared right now.

Over the next couple weeks, we did our best to process while also bracing ourselves for more change. Jesse was switching daycares again back to somewhere closer to us and Jeremiah was also going to be going with him. This was going to be a huge adjustment for everybody. I have never had a break from Jeremiah before, but I needed it! Plus, I was thinking about returning to work in the new year and needed daycare set up for that too.

CHAPTER 21
SEPTEMBER 2021
TAKING OFF RIDING

I had no expectations for September. I had learned by this point not to have any expectations of how the month "should" go. In the last year and a half, we have been given a baby, a pandemic, cancer (twice), and the death of my father-in-law. Having my second baby was my only "plan" for 2020. Now, I understand, truly what it means to trust God with our future because we really have no idea what it holds. God does know though, and He is there to watch over and protect me and help me grow through all of it.

We spent the last of the sunny summer days outside as much as possible. Jesse had been getting quite good at riding his pedal bike now and was even close to ready to take off his training wheels. I knew he was ready, but he wasn't quite sure. He kept saying, "Mom, I'll take my training wheels off when I'm four." I may have given an extra nudge when I told him he couldn't go as fast as me on my bike because his training wheels were slowing him down (which was true!). The next day he asked if we could take them off! We got them off and he was gone flying down the road and around the roundabout in our complex! I knew he was ready!

Three years old, and he was riding a pedal bike with no training wheels. I was so proud!

Three-year-old Jesse riding a pedal bike without training wheels

Labour day weekend rolled around, and Dave and I finally got a date day! Luke and Shelley offered to come watch Jesse and Jeremiah for us for a few hours so we could go out on a date — just the two of us! We decided to go see a movie in town. It was so nice to sit it a quiet theatre, eating snacks, and holding Dave's hand without any interruptions! I love our kids dearly but time away is just such a necessity for survival. I'm a better parent if I get that time away and I'm a better spouse. We saw an afternoon movie and then went for dinner. Again, our dinner experience was amazing. The table didn't come with crayons and a children's menu for one. And we got to finish every conversation we started! And oh, there were so many. Dave and I had been in a good place lately. I think we were both struggling in our own ways, but our marriage was strong, and we both had a lot of respect for each other. It was so nice to have this time to connect and spend some good quality time together.

As I was heading upstairs, my phone rang. Dave had it and saw it was our friend Julia. After hanging up Dave looked at me and said, "Good thing we have a spare bed." Julia currently had nowhere to go, and Dave and I were the first people to pop in her mind.

Knowing Julia thought of Dave and I right away made us extremely happy. We have always wanted our home to be a safe place, a haven, always open for a coffee, hug, or a bed to sleep on if our friends and family ever needed anything. To know that Julia thought of us brought us so much joy.

Julia got to our house just after 8:00 pm. Her living situation was not healthy and did not meet even the simplest of Julia's needs. It was one of those situations where you must get out first and then figure out your plan. We got Julia settled into her room equipped with a bed, TV, and a whole bunch of extra kids toys if she got bored! We went to bed that night praying that she felt safe here with us and that we would be able to just love on her and encourage her.

When it comes to our tithing money, we don't always give it to the church. We believe it is for God's people and not all of God's people are in the church. One morning I knew exactly where our tithing money was going. I had an appointment later that afternoon for a manicure and pedicure. It was part of my regular self-care that I had been doing all summer. I talked to Dave about it first, but I didn't even finish telling him everything when he said, "Do it." Of course, we were going to use our money to pay for Julia's manicure and pedicure. I invited her to come along, and she politely declined because of finances. I told her she didn't have to worry about it and that I had already talked to Dave. I explained this is what we do with our tithing money.

It wasn't putting us out or setting us back in the slightest. She happily agreed and I set the appointment.

It was nice having someone come with me that time to do my nails. We had good conversation, ranging from relationships, to mental health, Christianity, and more. I was really enjoying her company. We were in two totally different stages of life but at this time, we seemed good for each other.

I had just gotten a new bike, so I had an extra bike at this time. I invited her to go along with me on my evening bike ride to the river. Julia gladly accepted with a grin on her face. After the kids went to bed, we took off on our bikes and headed to the river. She did great. It was her first time on a bike in years. It was a gorgeous ride along the river. We got to Lickman Road, sat down and just talked for a while at this peaceful little stream flowing parallel to the river behind some trees. We sat there until the sun went down and then headed back home.

Over the course of the next two weeks, Julia spent days looking up jobs in the area and places to rent with no luck in either department. I reassured her that she had no reason to panic as we were not going to kick her out. Right now, she had a place to stay. It was nice having someone else around, especially since my mental health wasn't doing that well and isolation makes it worse.

As we came out of summer and entered fall, I felt like I was starting to fall apart again. I don't know what got into me, but I became so anxious and irritable all the time. There's a phrase when kids have a temper tantrum that they have "flipped their lid" as in they are unable to regulate themselves again. I felt like I was daily flipping my lid. I was constantly getting myself set off over one thing or another, usually having to do with the kids. Some days I felt like maybe I shouldn't have been a mom because I was not cut out for this.

As September came closer to an end, I started panicking about October coming. I had no reason to panic for October. It was our first Thanksgiving without my father-in-law and that would be hard, but it was also Jesse's birthday that same weekend and that was going be exciting. The excitement wasn't enough for me though. Something else was physically happening to me. I found myself getting worked up at the littlest things, as well as feeling hot and sweaty at the store because of minuscule reasons. Not being able to take my mask off in those moments proved to be extremely tricky, as my anxiety skyrockets when I feel like I already can't breathe. We still had the mask mandate in effect that required face masks to be worn in all indoor places, so it was the law unfortunately.

On top of my anxiety setting off at any given time of day, I was starting to physically brace myself for what to expect this season. This time last year, we were preparing for Dave to start cancer treatment. His first day was set for October 13th. This year, as we got closer and closer to October, I could feel the physical anxiety I felt last year. I felt like all my memories of last winter were visions of what to expect this winter.

This year, I had all last year's memories come flooding back into my mind with such overflowing force, it emotionally knocked me down. I found myself struggling to think about anything else, only October 13th and the winter that was about to unfold. In my head I knew it was crazy thinking. I knew this year was not going to be like that. I knew Dave was doing well. In fact, we had just been to see his cancer doctor, who said everything looked great! Why was my body reacting in such a ridiculous manner?

I had been spending all summer focusing on self-care. Throughout the previous winter, I gained so much weight, I was the heaviest I had ever been in my life. Through the spring and summer, I worked hard on self-care to help myself feel better about myself. I got my nails done every couple of weeks, I got my hair cut once a month, and I was practising eating better to try and lose the excess weight. By this point, I was down 55 pounds from my highest weight, and I felt amazing. One thing that was a huge aid was exercise by means of bike riding.

When I first started riding my bike, I wasn't sure if I could make it to my dad's house three kilometres away. As I worked my way through September, I started going on daily twenty-kilometre rides along the Vedder Rotary Trail at the River. With everything going on in my head, there was nothing like riding along the river and through the trails in between trees, rocks, and further nature. It was so freeing to be out on my bike. It was a true escape from my head, a therapeutic distraction.

Eventually the bike ride had to stop, and I had to return home. Even at twenty kilometres, as soon as I got to my home stretch, I could feel the anxiety return. I could feel myself feeling heartbroken my ride was done. I wanted to turn the bike around and do it all again. I never felt ready to come back home. I don't know why, there was nothing wrong with home. Dave and I were in a good place in our marriage, the kids were generally asleep or at daycare when

I did my rides, but something about coming home brought me back to my anxiety I had before departing on my ride. Unless I was riding, I just couldn't shake it.

I sent my psychiatrist an early morning plea one morning. I explained what was happening in life, and I told him what I had been experiencing. By the end of the two-page email, I begged him to help me. Something had to change. I later got a reply from the front desk saying my doctor had faxed a new prescription to my pharmacy, and he wanted me to start it that night. Whatever it was, I was desperate to try it.

Lately, everything had been a struggle. Getting up, getting the kids out the door, getting groceries, making meals, and the list goes on. Other than bike riding, I was not motivated to do anything. Watching shows and online shopping were my only interests when I couldn't be out on my bike. Everything else was too much work or caused me too much anxiety. I didn't know what was wrong with me. This felt different than my depression and anxiety in the past, but it was also so unsettling, I couldn't shake it.

On Tuesday, September 28th, I finally had an actual appointment with my psychiatrist. He explained to me that the new medication he prescribed before the weekend was for PTSD with which he had diagnosed me. He explained most people's brains process memories and move on simply calling it a memory. Some people, however, are unable to move beyond it and get stuck experiencing similar physical and emotional issues as when the trauma was experienced. In my case, I was physically and emotionally re-experiencing Dave's cancer treatment.

When the doctor first said PTSD, my jaw dropped. There's no way I have PTSD. Dave has PTSD. I do not have PTSD.

I struggle with anxiety and depression as part of having bipolar disorder, but I do not have PTSD. Upon further discussion with my psychiatrist though, I realized I was about to embark on a new journey learning and living through PTSD. I still didn't know how I felt about it though. What would this mean for me? What would it look like? Only time would tell for me. In the meantime, I go back to putting my trust in God trusting this is all part of His plan.

CHAPTER 22
OCTOBER 2021
TRAUMA-VERSARY

This year, Dave was healthy, both kids were in daycare, things were good. Yet, I couldn't let go of anything. Dave's cancer was always on my mind, always eating away at me. If I wasn't thinking about last year's treatment, I was worrying about the next time he might tell me about a lump. I couldn't accept this was over. It had been our life for so long. Every time Dave got a runny nose, a cough, a cold, a sore, or an ache, my heart would palpitate. I just had this feeling we weren't done this journey.

I did what I could to let go of the anxiety. I find the physical release is often the best way to relieve the "negative energy" I call it, so I tried my best to get it out through exercise as best I could. I was riding my bike 25km a day and walking the kids to daycare and back every day. I watched what I ate, I surrounded myself with positivity, but nothing was enough. My anxiety was getting the best of me.

I was lashing out at my kids and my husband for little things that were completely out of my control. I was giving my preschooler unclear and inconsistent boundaries which I knew was not okay. I was screaming at my screaming toddler to stop screaming which seemed totally conflicting and no wonder it didn't work. I had just lost myself. I always strive to do the best I can until I know better and then I can do better. I never wanted to slide back on the parenting scale, it just happened. "Have grace on yourself" was all I could keep telling myself, but it was hard. I felt like I was failing more and more every day.

A big part of taking care of myself was self-care, such as eating right, getting exercise, prayer, writing, friendship, and filling my bucket of needs. The other big part of taking care of myself was self-awareness. I had to know where I was at in my mental health. I can't get myself help if I didn't know what I needed. I can't always recognize when I am in a depression but if I pay enough attention, I can recognize the starting signs of a depression coming on. It probably looks a little different for everyone but for me, I generally start to open the Facebook app more. I spend less time praying, more time wasted scrolling through my phone. I tend to spend less time focussed on housework and tidiness, and more time watching shows. I lose the ambition to respond to messages when people send them. Often, it's days later, and it's not because I got busy. It's because I just didn't feel like responding.

My **Building Connections** ministry which I started in January had slowly been dwindling down to a message or two a day. That's how I knew I was in a depression this time. My intentions were there to message people, as I had been for the last ten months, but the motivation was not present. I found myself struggling to keep a conversation going. I was more interested in sitting on my phone or watching a show. This wasn't me. My anxiety was at one of the highest points it has been, since I was post-partum with my first born who was almost four. I knew I needed more help.

I had already reached out to my psychiatrist in desperation who increased one medication and started me on the other for PTSD at the end of September. I still felt I needed something more at this time. I messaged my psychiatrist office once again asking about a medication increase as well as contacted my counsellor at the BC Cancer Agency. I couldn't live with this anxiety anymore. It was eating me up daily. I couldn't focus on anything.

My thoughts were always drifting, my mind was always going, and my anxiety was always raging. It was only October, there were no signs of cancer, and though things were supposed to be "normal", this was nowhere near normal. I had been monitoring my mental health for over ten years by this point. I knew my normal. This was not normal for me. Circumstances may have been normal at that time, but I was far from. The worst part was, I had no idea what I needed.

Throughout my whole mental health journey, I have trained myself to become self-aware and realize what it is my body needs. Generally, when we have irritable moments, we can start by evaluating things like hunger, sleep, and downtime. With something like bipolar, it becomes slightly more complicated because many other factors can contribute to the ups and downs of the manic-depressive illness. With PTSD, it was even different. I couldn't figure out what it was that I needed, let alone be able to attain it. I could see Dave was checking out again which showed he didn't know what he needed either.

I think the only thing I could handle was getting myself through each day five minutes at a time. Just as I rode my bike one kilometre at a time, I lived my days one section at a time. Sometimes that section was five minutes of raging anxiety I thought would take me down. Sometimes it was two hours of blissful bike riding so satisfying, I felt peace would never leave me again. Being out on my bike was so good for me. It gave me the freedom from my brain that I needed, and I used many opportunities to help me see physical life lessons.

One thing I did when I went on my 20-kilometre Vedder Rotary Loop was stop at every single km marker along the way every single time. The first time I stopped to take a photo of myself at every marker and now I still stop every time. Why do I do this? It's a physical reminder to myself to stop before I feel myself wearing out. I stop every kilometre to evaluate what it is I am needing. Sometimes I need some water, sometimes I need to get off my bike and stretch my legs, and yeah sometimes I need a selfie! You know why? Because I am so dang proud of myself!

Bike selfie after a 20km ride

Finding the power to be proud of myself during these days was tough! I certainly did not feel proud of myself at home. At home, I felt like I was the worst person for my family to be around. I was reactive and on edge most of the time. I loved my husband and kids very much and we were all close but something about where my head was at now, I just didn't want people. I finally understood where Dave's head has been all these years struggling with PTSD. I get that he doesn't feel like he has the capabilities to do much other than basic survival. I feel like that.

My current capabilities were keeping the kids alive and planning Jesse's birthday which fell on Thanksgiving Sunday that year. This would be the first Thanksgiving without Dave's dad, and it was going to be a hard one. Luckily, with it being Jesse's birthday, we hoped it would lighten the mood.

On the morning of Jesse's birthday, I think I was probably more excited than him. Jesse woke up shortly after 5:00am as usual, came downstairs and immediately asked, "Mom, what is all that doing up like that?" He's so funny, he must know why everything is the way it is before he can accept it and enjoy it. Once I told him I decorated for his birthday and told him he was four, he came running down the stairs! He went straight for the pile of balloons on the living room floor, then he saw his present. He opened it up, saw it was a new scooter, shrieked out the word "YES!" and then said, "This is the perfect present." I don't think I have ever felt so proud of a gift. My four-year-old, who speaks only truth at this age tells me I bought him the perfect present.

I was feeling the anxiety about the week already, but I tried not to show it to my boys. I wanted to be strong for them as hard as that was. I get showing weakness and being vulnerable can be a good thing, but I also didn't want to scare my sons. When my anxiety gets the best of me, I start overreacting and acting irrational about things that really shouldn't matter. I always take the time to self-reflect later but, in the moment, it's hard to bring myself back. And then the mom guilt eats me alive.

The mom guilt eating me alive was only the tip of the iceberg for what had been bothering me and eating me up. I kept reliving Dave's cancer treatment, feeling in the depth of my soul we weren't done this journey. Jeremiah had been sick again which made me worry even more about him and the possibility of him having cancer. He was the only one in the house getting these fever flare ups and yet he and his brother were together at the same daycare. Jesse wasn't getting sick, not like Jeremiah was. My anxiety was crippling, my depression was setting in, and I felt like crawling into a cave until spring. Of course, being a mom, I can't escape from my responsibilities, nor could I escape my head.

I sent another plea to my doctor as soon as I started noticing my depression set in. I was losing interest in everything with the kids, I didn't feel like eating anything at all, I started napping during the day, and I found myself checking out more often that I had ever before. I lost interest in writing, I lost interest in **Building Connections**, I even lost interest in smiling. It was simply too much effort.

I knew I needed more help, so I reached out again to my counsellor at the Abbotsford Cancer Centre. I hadn't heard back from her, and I knew I needed to talk to someone. I sent an email message to her and a heaven message to God asking desperately for some extra strength. I don't remember the last time I had felt so vulnerable.

One thing I have to say about PTSD I wasn't used to, were the flashbacks that vividly flashed across my mind. They were almost as if I was there again when the trauma first happened. It was so frustrating when it was the most mundane task that sent me into extreme anxiety. One day, I had to empty out the rotting fridge food. Now, Dave and I have a mutual agreement in our marriage. Anything to do with poop or vomit is for me to take care of, and anything to do with rotting food is him. One day, the kids and I did a substantial grocery shop for Jesse's birthday party. I had no room in the fridge to put everything because of all the containers of food Dave forgot to empty. No big deal, I was sure I could suck it up and push through it. What's a little rotting gravy and mashed potatoes?

What got to me was not how gross the gravy and mashed potatoes were but how I felt my body react to pulling out the food. As soon as I grabbed the first container to pull it out, I got this vivid vision of pulling out containers from the fridge last year when Dave was in the hospital. This year when I was pulling out the food and pouring it into the bags, I could physically see myself doing it last year, I could feel the anxiety in my body and I cried my way through it, telling myself it was only a memory, Dave was fine now. As I walked the compost bag down my inside stairs to the garage, I could again see myself walking up the outside stairs at our old house to bring all the bags to the compost. I could almost feel the rain beading on my housecoat as I ran it up as quick as I could in my slippers. This year, I didn't even have to go outside, and yet I had the same reaction, if not worse, than last year.

My counsellor told me that is a normal trauma response

for someone with PTSD. She explained that last year, my body was not in a safe place to process and properly handle the emotions which were flooding my mind. Last year, I did what I needed to do to get through it. Now that things were going well and I was in a safe place mentally, my body was "dealing" with what it should have dealt with last year. I couldn't understand why I was having these reactions and PTSD when Dave was the one that went through cancer. My counsellor also explained that was perfectly normal as well. She said, typically it is the caregiver of the one going through cancer who struggles the most afterward.

Hearing my counsellor tell me it was typical for the caregiver to struggle more after, was music to my soul. It wasn't that I wanted to struggle by any means. I wanted to be normal. But hearing that made me feel extremely heard and validated. It helped make more sense in my head to hear this was normal. I knew I was still going to struggle but at least now, I understood why I was struggling. My next plan of action was to contact Chilliwack Mental Health and see about seeking some counselling resources through them. Erin was amazing but she was specific for patients dealing with cancer trauma. Although this was in fact, cancer trauma, Dave had been finished with treatment for nearly a year. I wasn't going to be able to continue using the cancer centre resources for too many more sessions.

I planned to contact Chilliwack Mental Health. In the meantime, I spoke with my psychiatrist who was temporarily putting me on Ativan to try and calm me before Halloween. Halloween was a huge trigger for me. Last year I had a bit of a breakdown out front my house on Halloween night. I missed out on taking Jesse trick or treating and fell apart because Dave was too weak to walk down the road. I remember it vividly like it was yesterday. Missing out on taking Jesse trick or treating for the first year he would remember, was devastating. I can feel the tension in my body just thinking about missing out on taking him. To some, it may be no big deal, but we struggled to have kids for so long, this was a rite of passage I waited for and deserved to do with my son.

Halloween was finally here, and I didn't know how I felt about it. I was hopeful new emotions would accompany my existing fears and anxieties. I was hopeful we would enjoy a fun family event trick or treating through the neighbourhood together. By Sunday morning though, my hopes were starting to be taken over by fears and anxieties yet again.

This year, my fears and anxieties were not only related to Dave's previous cancer treatment but the health of my 16-month-old baby Jeremiah. He had been sick in August and some concerning bloodwork pointed in the direction of bone marrow cancer. Obviously, my anxiety skyrocketing at that time and has not quite come back down. One thing the doctor told me to look out for was reoccurring infections. Since August he had four fever flare ups all mimicking the same symptoms as the first one in August. I didn't take him into the hospital, but I did call the paediatrician and treat the fever at home. On Halloween day, he got his fifth fever flare up resulting in the breaking of my anxiety window of tolerance.

Seeing him flare up again, on Halloween of all days, sent me into a whirlwind of emotion. I needed answers and I needed them now. I couldn't keep going through this.

I decided to take him straight to the children's hospital in Vancouver where they specialize in treatment for kids who have cancer and other medical issues. I figured that is where I needed to be.

Jeremiah's fever was all over the place, and I couldn't predict when it was going to jump over 104F again. The drive to the Children's Hospital was an hour and a half away. I prayed my baby boy would peacefully sleep at just the right temperature so to not overheat in the van. I know I have had a lot of anxiety in the past nearly two years, but this was anxiety at its peak. I was about to walk into a door and possibly find out if my baby had cancer. Were we really going to do cancer again in our family and so soon?

I arrived at BC Children's hospital shortly before 4:00pm, riddled with anxiety. I wished Dave could be here with me, but he had to take Jesse trick or treating like we were all supposed to go. I still couldn't believe I was going to miss it… again. But this was more important. We needed answers and we needed them now. My anxiety couldn't go another day wondering what was going to happen next. I grabbed my sick baby boy and headed towards the door, mask in hand. "God help me through this" I whispered, as I walked through the front doors of the hospital emergency room.

I waited with Jeremiah in the stroller for the good part of two hours until they were ready for him. Finally at six o'clock, they called Jeremiah's name. My nerves were sky high again. We would hopefully get our answers tonight. I trusted God with all of it as I followed the nurse down the hall to room 117. Once we got inside the room, my anxieties started to ease instantly. It was a nice room, private, with a sliding door to block out the hallway noise.

The nurse didn't waste any time. Her questions started with when the fever started, what other symptoms he had, and what I had given him for it. His fever at that time had been going up and down so I didn't know what to expect. She used her forehead thermometer which took no time to start beeping. Jeremiah's fever was at 102.5F, the poor guy. The nurse brought him some Tylenol and Advil and told me she would come back in about an hour to assess him again. In the meantime, she told me to push water as much as I could.

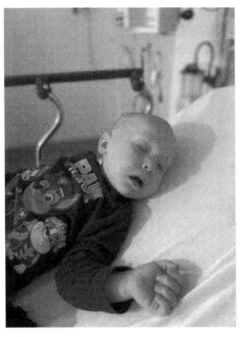

Jeremiah in Children's Hospital

After an hour went by, the doctor came by and looked at my little Jeremiah. She asked me a few questions about what happened in August and then explained to me what happened from her perspective. She said Jeremiah had some concerning bloodwork which needed to be followed up. The other doctor in August explained to me cancer was a concern. This doctor at Children's explained that although the lab work had some significant red flags, the doctor should never have used the word cancer until we knew more. She also went on to explain the follow up bloodwork came back better showing it was a virus causing his cell levels to drop so significantly. She said if he had cancer, his levels would likely stay depleted.

One thing I've held onto is our verse for his name, Jeremiah 29:11. It talks about giving us a hope and a future based on his plan for us. The hope and future the Bible is talking about is not necessarily our current future on earth. Yes, he does give us hope here on earth and he does prepare our future but for what? For a heaven bound future glorifying him.

So why not start glorifying him now? I hold onto that verse for my sweet boy, not because I think it means God will keep him from cancer. I hold onto that verse because God is promising me hope and his eternal future. He is speaking of his good plan. His plan is so interconnected on so many levels; if Jeremiah did have cancer one day, it likely wouldn't even be about him. It could be about someone else affected by Jeremiah's cancer. It could be about the people watching our story. It could be about the nurses at the hospital caring for him. It could be about so many more things than our little minds are capable of understanding. But that's the beauty of God's plan, it's His! We don't need to worry about it, we just need to trust in it and trust that it is ultimately for good.

CHAPTER 23

NOVEMBER 2021

NATURAL DISASTERS

Starting off November was hard. Jeremiah had just been sick in the hospital, Jesse then got sick with what Jeremiah had, and my PTSD was putting me in a bad place. Plus, my dad, who I had grown close with, was moving up north this month. I didn't know how I would figure out life without him. He had been such a staple in my life since the pandemic, I didn't know quite what to do with him so far away. It was approaching Christmas, my mental health wasn't well, and things just didn't feel right.

I felt like we were never going to be finished Dave's cancer. Yes, he was cancer free now, but would that always be the case? Would my mind ever let go of the fears of cancer returning? And what about the issues which were still ongoing? Because of the radiation on Dave's mouth, it destroyed all his teeth. This meant, over the next number of months, Dave would need multiple dental surgeries to remove all the teeth in his mouth. Once they were all removed, he could be fitted for dentures but in the meantime, it's yet another loss.

One thing I looked forward to was moving my dad to Clinton, three hours away. I was so sad to see him move away as we had grown so close, but I was excited to help with the move there and have a bit of a break from home. My anxiety had been getting the best of me lately and it just wasn't good for anybody in our house. I needed the break.

On November 10th, my dad and Kim, their friend Bill, and myself all made the three-hour drive to Clinton. We spent the next three days unpacking, and then Dave and the kids came up on the 13th. I enjoyed my break, but I was so happy to see my family again. I really missed them! Dave and the kids were spending the night and we were heading out Sunday morning. The only thing we had to worry about now was the weather.

Come Sunday morning, the weather had changed from beautiful sunny skies to rainy and overcast with high amounts of expected rain. We headed out around ten o'clock and made it all the way through Spences Bridge, to Boston Bar before we were stopped. There was a rockslide at Yale tunnel, blocking us from getting through. We looked at rerouting through the Coquihalla but there was a mudslide there blocking traffic both directions. The only thing we could do was turn around and go back to my dad's, the two-hour drive back. By the time we got back to my dad's, we found out major parts of the highway at Spences Bridge were wiped out. They were wiped right out, as in gone completely. It was horrific to see and a little traumatizing to know we drove through that area not once but twice that day trying to get home!

The plan was to get going first thing the next morning, November 15th, and take highway 99 through Whistler to get home. That would take about six hours but at least it would take us home. We were all ready by 7:30 and thought it was best to just hit the road. We had a long drive ahead of us and the weather was not on our side. So far, two of the three routes home were washed out by mudslides and rockslides. We didn't want to take any chances with highway 99, our only route back home. It was time to go.

The rain was really coming down and the roads were not in good condition. I made a plea on Facebook asking for prayers as we needed to take highway 99 through the treacherous roads filled with rain and snow. When we mapped the route, it was now saying seven hours to get home. We said our goodbyes and headed out, praying for God to keep us safe.

The plan was to drive to Lillooet to take a short break and then head through Pemberton and Whistler, before finding our familiar route along the Highway One in Vancouver. Due to kids, we needed another break in Squamish. We made it through the worst of the terrible road conditions and now it was time to take a breather. We stopped by the local grocery store and picked up some produce for the kids and used the facilities. While we were there, I thought I would open Facebook to update anyone who was praying for our safe travels. While checking Facebook, my jaw dropped.

I came across an article and had to re-read it three times before showing Dave in disbelief. There were officially no routes into Vancouver from the interior. Highway 99 was the last available route and a deadly mudslide had just wiped it out. I clicked on the article to read that shortly after 11am, a mudslide had wiped across the road taking out everything in its path. This happened between Lillooet and Pemberton. I have a video on my phone of us going through that area at

10:36am! We missed the mudslide by less than half an hour! God was watching out for us!

The rain was picking up heavier than I had ever seen it before, it was getting scary. By the time we got into Abbotsford heading to Chilliwack, the water was starting to pile on the side of the freeway. It looked like the freeway was going to get washed out. The roads on either side of the freeway were both under water. If the water levels came up any higher, the freeway would be under water too. We just needed to make it home before that happened.

We crossed back into Chilliwack around 4 o'clock. We later found out the freeway was shut down by 5:30 due to flowing water travelling across it. This was crazy. Cars were left on the side of the freeway unable to continue driving. People had driven into the centre because they couldn't see where the road ended, and the ditch began. The worst part was the rain just kept on coming and there was no end in sight. We were expecting 100mm at one time!

Over the next few days, we were trapped in Chilliwack. Between flooding, rockslides, and mudslides wiping out so many routes throughout BC, we couldn't go anywhere. Highway One to Agassiz was closed, Highway Seven was closed both directions, and Highway One to Abbotsford was completely submerged by water. I had never felt more trapped and wanting to leave more than I did now. Things just weren't the same.

A lot of things hadn't been the same lately. I don't know if it was the flooding, or my PTSD, the season, or something else, but I just wasn't myself. I had fallen in this slump, unable to pull myself out despite my best efforts.

I prayed to God to keep me from it, but for some reason,

my returning depression was part of God's plan.

I have struggled with depression many times in my life. In my past, it looked a little different than it does now. When I think about depression in my past, I see suicidal thoughts, self-harm, and not being able to get out of bed in the morning. Now, as I have a bit more experience, knowledge, and a toolbox of skills, I am better able to handle myself when depression strikes. I know the things to do and not to do to aid in its journey. It's not something I can make go away but I can help control the symptoms as best I can.

Knowing about depression and having the necessary skills to deal with it has saved my life. To think back that there was a time depression made me want to truly die because I was so hopeless. I didn't know if there would ever be a time that I would feel better again, or normal. I didn't know how to treat depression or how to take care of myself in depression. I just sunk deeper and deeper each day. Today I can understand depression more and see it isn't going to last forever and yes, I will feel better one day. It is a period, however long it may be, and then it will pass.

I see depression now as having a cold, a nasty cold sometimes, but a cold, nonetheless. You can't always stop it from happening, but you can treat the symptoms. A cold might last a few days, a few weeks, or sometimes a bad one might have you down for a few months. The more you know about colds, the more you can treat one. Whether it's by cold medication, self-care and rest, adequate food, or a Costco size box of Kleenex, we know what we can expect when we get a cold and we can brace ourselves for the ride.

Dealing with depression now is still hard. I have the skills, I have the knowledge, I have the experience, but some days it doesn't feel like it's enough. I must remember to have grace on myself and be kind to myself. I must lower my expectations of myself and remember it is just a season, it won't last forever. I will find a new normal again, and in the meantime, I will cope and continue living my life adapting to the fact depression is now my shadow again.

The flooding was still an ongoing issue. The weather forecasters were expecting up to 125mm of rain over the weekend and nobody knew exactly how that was going to affect the prairies and the freeway and anywhere else that was just getting its grounds back. The flooding on November 15th had all of Sumas Prairie under water. What was another 125mm of rain going to do? The freeway had just opened on November 25th, but I feared this amount of rain would shut it down again.

I was really hoping to get out to Abbotsford the following week for Jesse's appointment. He had been struggling with many things for the last number of years and by the age of two, I started to suspect autism. He had some "quirks" I called them, and as he got older, the quirks became more challenging behaviours. He went on a wait list for an autism assessment in October of 2019, and that assessment was next week! I just hoped we could make it, so we didn't have to reschedule for the following year. I needed answers. I was a desperate parent looking for ways to help my son through an already difficult time. I felt so bad for him, but I was also anxious about this pending diagnosis.

I had part one of the assessment via zoom on Monday November 15th while driving home from Clinton. I was sitting in the back seat answering the doctor's questions as seriously as I could while turning my phone to show her the boats driving down North Parallel Road. It was the most bizarre appointment I have had thus far. In all seriousness though, the appointment went well. I felt extremely validated and was ready to have the next appointment. Now that it was approaching though, I was feeling scared, nervous, and apprehensive. I started thinking about what this would mean. It was one thing to have my suspicions but to have a diagnosis was a whole new story. To say my son has autism are words I honestly didn't hear myself saying.

Now as we moved into December, I had Jesse's pending autism assessment, Dave's first of many dental surgeries, and my depression was setting in. I felt like we were in for a rough month but at the same time I was choosing to trust God with all of it. Jesse's autism assessment was in God's hands, Dave's teeth were in God's hands, and my depression and PTSD were in God's hands. Whether I liked having it or not, it was all part of the master plan.

CHAPTER 24

DECEMBER 2021

CHANGE AND A NEW YEAR

December... the most cheerful month of the year? The current flooding had many without homes and more rain was expected. I was depressed and struggling with PTSD, Jesse was in the process of being diagnosed with autism, and Dave was about to lose all his teeth. I didn't know where the cheer would fit in, but I tried to be optimistic. This December had to be better than last year, right?

Friday December 3rd was a hard day. It marked one year since Dave completed his cancer treatment. You would think this would be a joyful day, a day to celebrate the health of Dave now. For some reason unknown to myself, I was triggered by it. It was the first day the freeway was open, my kids were in daycare, and I sat at home all day. I didn't have the motivation to do anything but scroll through Facebook and listen to meditation music. I knew I needed to do something about this depression, so I talked to my doctor about increasing my medication and moving one of my evening medications to the morning. My doctor gladly obliged and told me to call the office a week before Christmas if I wasn't feeling better.

I love the support I have from my doctor when it comes

to my mental health. I think the relationship you have with your doctor is so important. You want to know your doctor has your best interest at heart, and I know mine does. I even talked to him about returning to work next month and he was supportive of it. It had been two years since I was off work and a lot had changed in the world, in me. I wasn't sure if I was ready. I wasn't sure how work life would go. Lately I had been struggling in my mom life so adding something new was scary.

    Lately I had been struggling so bad with my depression and my PTSD, that my mom journey didn't look anything like I thought it would. Before I had kids, I envisioned myself being hands-on all day long, doing arts, games, and science experiments. The reality? They watch a lot of tv, and I sit a lot and watch them play. I just don't want to get down on the floor to play, I don't want to pull out the art stuff, I really don't want to clean up the mess from making play dough or slime. It was just easier to let them watch a show and play by themselves. But it wasn't ideal.

    Daycare days were my saving grace. I felt extreme guilt for sending them to daycare because I had the expectation of myself that I "should" be doing everything with my kids. The truth is, I shouldn't feel guilty for sending them to daycare because they are being loved on. It's not that I don't love on them because I do, but when I'm not well, I can't be the best parent I know I am capable of being. Therefore, it is okay to pass on the responsibilities to someone else temporarily. Besides, my kids love daycare. When I unbuckle Jeremiah at daycare, he can't wait to bust out of his seat and run inside. I don't even get a goodbye from him.

    Since Jeremiah was 18 months old now, it meant my

maternity leave was over. Back in January of 2020, I was struggling with my depression but was also pregnant and my baby was struggling too. My doctor removed me from work for the remainder of my pregnancy to which I went on an 18-month maternity leave. Was I ready to go back? I had certainly been through a lot in the last two years, but I thought work would be a good place for me. It could be a place where I can separate myself from what's around me at home. I said yes to returning and was set to start on January 10th. In the meantime, we just had to take care of Dave's teeth, Christmas, and Jesse's autism assessment.

Dave's first of many tooth extractions was happening on December 6th. This was a hard day for him. He had already lost so much from his cancer treatment, now he was losing his teeth too. I asked him one day, "What is the hardest part about losing your teeth?" He looked at me and said, "My self-confidence". He also said, "Eating has been very frustrating, and one of the biggest ones is it's a daily reminder that cancer is still taking a toll on me." It was hard to move on with everything else in life when there was always a daily reminder that cancer has played a very real part.

Jesse's autism assessment was finally here, although that morning we all woke up to our world covered in snow! It has snowed through the night and continued during the morning affecting the morning commuters. I was super anxious about making it so Abbotsford, so I dropped Jeremiah off early and hit the freeway which had just recently opened again. I worried with all this snow; it might close. I knew for the sake of Jesse's appointment, if the road closed, I wanted to be on the other end.

I remember walking into the appointment just trembling,

thinking this was it. This was where we were going to find out what has been going on with our Jesse. I got the honor of doing more paperwork while the doctor and Jesse went and "played" together in a room. The appointment was 90 minutes long and Jesse did great. He cooperated and even had fun! I was so thrilled.

The results for Jesse's assessment were set for December 9th. I sat by the computer ready to go and at 2:00 pm exactly, the doctor joined the zoom call. She started by explaining all the reasons we initially went ahead with wanting an autism assessment. She explained the reasons the doctor made the referral and the reasons I made my referral. She explained what she saw in her assessment of Jesse and what she observed in him over the hour and a half long assessment. Her findings were that yes, he did meet the criteria for autism in a few different categories. My son… has autism.

To hear the words were just so shocking. This was no longer Jesse displaying some curious quirks, it was a lifelong disability. I had a lifelong disability, so I understood what this meant… it was a lifetime. There is absolutely nothing wrong with having a lifelong disability, but it comes with its many challenges. For me, I have bipolar disorder. For my entire life, I must watch and monitor myself closely and watch for highs and lows in my mood. For Jesse, he will have autism for his entire life and although he won't have to watch for his highs and lows, he will have to learn to adapt to the things that make him feel uncomfortable. For a child (or adult) with autism, that individual has certain challenges that pertain to their everyday lives. As Jesse gets older, those challenges will require more support for him as well as for us as we navigate raising a child on the spectrum.

Getting the diagnosis was such a process. It took two years, going through covid, cancer, rain, wind, and snow to get it done but it was finally done and now we know... except we're not done. This is only the beginning. Now we had to set up services for him, I had to prepare for returning to work, and Dave was in the process of losing all his teeth.

There was a lot of the cancer journey that we were both still grieving and mourning. I find it weird to use those words but my counsellor at the BC Cancer Agency has used them regularly with me over the last two years. I always questioned her asking how I can grieve and mourn if Dave didn't die? She explained to me there were a lot of things I did lose, and it was important to validate those losses. I feel like I missed out on Jeremiah's whole first year of life because of cancer. I feel so guilty about it, my heart races every time I think about it. Dave is losing his teeth; Jesse nearly lost his dad. For weeks last Christmas, we thought we would lose him. I am still very affected by cancer. We all are. I don't think it is something that will ever leave us, but I hope with time, it will get easier.

Christmas was fast approaching, and I felt ready/not ready if you know what I mean. I was done with my shopping, I had done my wrapping, the house was decorated, Dave had been into his annual baking, and the countdown was on. However, ten days to go before Christmas and all I kept thinking about was when Christmas would be over. I just wasn't into it this year. I was more interested in thinking about how I was going to reorganize the house once all the Christmas stuff was put away... hopefully in ten days.

When we woke up on Christmas morning, we woke up

to a winter wonderland, and it was beautiful! The snow started falling first thing in the morning and didn't stop all day long. The snow, combined with arctic winds though, created a problem for us who needed to travel to Abbotsford. The Sumas flats was a bad area to drive in the winter and unfortunately, the freeway goes right through it. It was recommended to all drivers out there, only travel if it is essential. The roads were terrible, and it wasn't worth risking safety to go have a meal together. Because of this, we stayed home Christmas day and had appetizers trying to celebrate this Christmas together. We were thankful we chose safety, but it was hard not to be with the extended family.

New Year's was around the corner. I think everyone was a little apprehensive about this New Year's. The last two years have consisted of this pandemic, raging forest fires, heat domes, atmospheric rivers, and everything in between. We were mentally done with the weather, we were exhausted with the pandemic, and we were ready to start a new year.

One thing that has helped me throughout this crazy year has been my self-care journey. Through having two young kids and carrying such a heavy load, it was easy to let myself fall on the back burner as I was busy carrying for everybody else's needs. What I really needed to learn was how to take care of myself. In 2021, I learned how to do that. Not that I turned selfish, but I learned the art of self-care. There's a big difference. I stopped adding so much cream and sugar to my coffee, I stopped going through drive throughs, and I began bike riding to help release some of the negative energy building up over the course of the pandemic. Throughout the next number of months, I started losing weight and began gaining confidence.

Photo comparison of Jenelle between May and December 2021

As December came to an end, I was down 80 pounds, had gained self-confidence, and learned how to love and appreciate myself because of learning self-care. I highly recommend starting your own journey of self-care because the rewards are worth it. I feel amazing now. I can keep up with my young kids without carrying around their equivalency of weight on me. I can walk around with a smile on my face knowing I am doing the best thing for myself I can. I can also better take care of those around me when I am taking care of myself.

It's so important to take care of ourselves so we are better able to take on caring for others. My little family has gone through so much the last couple years. There's no way I could care for everyone if I didn't care for myself. I need to make sure I eat right, get in my daily exercise, encourage those around me, and assess what my needs are regularly. Just like when I ride my bike, I stop every so often before I feel burnt out, to determine what my needs are. It's so important to stop and care for our needs before we feel burnt out. Once we're burnt out, we lose the ability to be self-aware and cannot determine what our needs even are.

Here's my encouragement to you. Start a journey of self-care. Take some time to determine what it is you need. Do you need to eat better? Do you need your first haircut in years? Do you need to start writing? Do you need to pick up a bicycle and experience the wind blowing through your hair? Do you need to learn how to love on yourself too? The self-care journey is worth it!

CHAPTER 25

TALKING ABOUT BUILDING CONNECTIONS

Through 2020 and 2021, my family and I faced trial after trial. I believe God allows the struggles to come to build up our strength, our character, and our determination to fight for life, for Him. We are called to live for Jesus, but how easy it is to say that we do and then turn around and live just for ourselves? Living for Jesus is to spend our lives glorifying Him through our words and our loving deeds for those who need them. We cannot love people with godly love unless we make a deep human connection. It is good for them, and it turns out to be exceptionally good for us, too. (God really leads us to what we need!)

We are not meant to do it alone. We are meant to be raising our kids together, we are meant to be worshipping and praising God together, we are meant to help each other and build each other up together. It takes the village of those around you whether believers of God or not. During the 2020/2021 pandemic, I found my village and I encourage you to find yours too. Ask God to direct you to where your most important needs can be met. Connection with people can look so many ways. During my rough season, my community of people around me were there for me in all the ways a village can be. I had friends who offered to grab me groceries when they went to the store. I had friends who came to help me clean my kitchen. I had family take Jesse on weekends when I was too overwhelmed. I had family take my laundry and wash it for me. I survived and I firmly believe I survived because of my faith in God who promises to provide, and because of my community of people standing beside me.

I still run my ministry that I started at the beginning of January 2021, and I call it **"Building Connections"**. It is my goal to reach out to as many people as I can and just simply encourage. Sometimes I send a picture of my kids, sometimes I randomly type someone and say, "Happy Friday" (or any other day of the week), and sometimes I just like to check on someone and ask how they are doing. Sometimes, I feel God putting friends on my heart, so I spend time first praying for that person. Then I message them and explain that I was thinking of them and/or praying for them. It's amazing what that can do to lift someone's day.

I remember the first time someone told me they had prayed for me, and it always brings me a smile to think about! I was finishing up my ECE schooling while working at a daycare back in 2009. One afternoon, my friend and I were walking into work together. She looked at me and asked me about the exam I had earlier that day. I remember telling her I got an A with a big smile on my face. The smile was returned as she said, "Oh that's amazing Jenelle, I was praying for you." I remember my jaw dropping. In my mind, it was only a test. It wasn't like someone was sick and dying or someone lost a job. It was just a test. To me it was just a test but to her, it was worth praying about. We weren't even that close yet at that time and she still took time out of her day to pray for her co-worker's test. I can't tell you how important that made me feel and how much that built me up. That is my goal with **Building Connections**.

Now I take the time to ask my friends how they are, and I take the time to pray for them. I may not have the ability to be as hands on help with two kids, but I can help by means of encouragement or offering to pick up groceries. I can help by ordering them a meal. I can help by assuring them that they are in my prayers and our prayers go straight to our Heavenly Father. When we bring a need to our father, the Bible says he will provide for that need. Philippians 4:19 in the new living translation says, "And this same God who takes care of me will supply all your needs from his glorious riches, which have been given to us in Christ Jesus." I want this to be the encouragement I give to others. God took care of me. He brought us through a dark time, and I firmly believe I can use this to encourage those around me.

I still struggle with things in my day-to-day life, and one thing that helps in my **Building Connections** ministry is being vulnerable. I can't know how to pray for my friends if they are not open with me. I also can't be helped and encouraged if I am not open with those around me. When I strike up my conversations with my friends, I try to make sure I am open and vulnerable because I really believe that builds a friendship too. Allowing our friends to see the side of us that struggles is good for a relationship. Of course, we don't want to overwhelm our friends with our burdens on a constant basis, but to be open and honest is a good start in any conversation.

Throughout my time with **Building Connections**, I have

come across so many times where I have talked to just the right person who said just the right thing that I needed to hear that day. There are times alternatively, where a friend will be going through a particular struggle, and I am the perfect person to talk to about it.

Now, a year later, I still build connections on a daily basis and I plan to keep it up. I have gotten to know so many wonderful people this year through my ministry and I have been able to encourage those around me as well. Next year, I hope to continue with **Building Connections** and maybe expand it beyond my circle of people. Why not use God's love and compassion to encourage the world? There are so many people out there who need a little encouragement, prayer, or just a spontaneous happy Friday text message. It is my goal to expand **Building Connections** and encourage others to try building their own connections through their community.

CHAPTER 26

TALKING ABOUT MENTAL HEALTH

When I first began my mental health struggle, I was in high school. There, I had no idea what was happening to me. I just didn't feel "right." Into my adolescence, my struggles continued, causing me pain and anguish everywhere I turned. I lost jobs, I lost relationships, I lost myself all because of something I didn't understand. I desperately tried to regain my balance on my own, but it seemed hopeless. I spiraled out of control into the depths of depression. Time and time again, I found myself in the care of doctors at various hospitals while I navigated this new thing called "mental health." I had a disorder and I had to learn to live with it.

In the beginning, when I first began learning about my mental health, I took part in various groups and programs available through the local mental health services. I joined a group on learning about depression. I took a group on learning about anxiety. I took a group for survivors of abuse because that was part of my past.

The more I went and took part in these programs, the more I learned and realized there wasn't anything wrong with me. I didn't stand out from everyone else.

There were many others who were there with me in those groups also looking for ways to challenge their own thinking. There, we all stood together and began the journey of learning how to care for ourselves.

Learning to care for myself looks different depending on where I am in life. When I was younger, I really got into colouring, journaling, and various other meditating exercises ranging from workbooks to guided meditation CD's. Sometimes I still find myself in a place where I need to meditate, or I need to sit down and do some colouring. I often have piano music going in the background at home. I still journal and I likely always will. There is something about writing and getting things out that is so refreshing for the soul. Exercise is a big one for me now. If I don't exercise, I drastically notice my mental health decline. Whatever I can do in a day to raise my heartbeat even just a little, it all counts.

Over the years, as I have learned how to care for myself, I have also learned the art of self-awareness. It can be challenging to know what you need if you don't know where you are currently at in your mental health journey. It is always a good idea for care for yourself but being self-aware is different. It involves doing a regular inventory of your body. It requires the ability to recognize when we are feeling off and do something about it rather than make excuses. A decade ago, I would typically say something like "I did this because of my depression or anxiety" or "I am this way because I have bipolar disorder." I can be a certain way because I have an illness, or I can be self-aware and realize where my needs are different than those around me. I need more support with my children and that is okay. I need medication to help balance my mood and that is okay. I need ongoing counselling and that is okay. All these things are put into place for me to live my life the fullest I can live WITH my mental health.

Today I live a very normal and balanced life. Those around me would never know I live a lifelong struggle. It's not that I keep it hidden, in fact I am very open and honest about it. I just don't let it control me like it used to. It would take me down every chance it got but now I am stronger than it. I am above it and I can stand tall today and proudly say I am in control of my mental health; it does not control me. I still struggle daily but being self-aware and giving myself self-care takes me where I need to go on this daily journey. I encourage you to find one thing you can do for yourself for self-care today.

CHAPTER 27

TALKING ABOUT CANCER

When Dave first went to his doctor about the sore in his mouth, we were never in a million years expecting to hear the word cancer that day. It was a word that changed our whole lives. There's something about hearing that word that makes your whole world shift. If there's anything in the world that makes you stop and think like that, it's the word cancer.

Dave's cancer was called "squamous cell carcinoma". It was in the inside of his mouth the first time and in his neck the second time. Squamous cell carcinoma is a skin cancer that develops in the squamous cells that make up the inner and outer layer of the skin. Most people will notice a sore or scab somewhere on their body that won't heal for a couple of months. If you have any sort of sore that won't heal, I highly recommend talking to your doctor about it. You just never know what it could be.

The first time Dave had cancer; it was able to be cured by surgery. The surgeon removed all the infected area and then did a biopsy on all the surrounding skin around the infection. If all the outside skin is benign, which Dave's was, then you are in the clear and need no further treatment.

Routine check-ups are required for the next number of years as reoccurrence is always possible. It's best to stay on top of it in case it does return.

Unfortunately, Dave's cancer returned just five months after his surgery. The surgeon attempted surgery again but was unsuccessful as the tumour had ruptured. This meant that Dave needed further treatment beyond surgery. The surgeon told Dave he would need 35 sessions of radiation as well as the surgery.

Radiation therapy is a cancer treatment that uses high doses of radiation to kill cancer cells and shrink tumours. There are many side effects of radiation ranging from skin changes to fatigue. Radiation treatment is targeted at one specific area, in Dave's case, his neck. Another side effect Dave still struggles with is his inability to make his own saliva. The radiation killed all cells responsible for creating saliva. This means he now needs a constant supply of water on hand before he gets so dry it hurts.

Because Dave's tumour spread to the other side of his neck, it meant he also needed chemotherapy. Chemotherapy is another cancer treatment that uses powerful chemicals to kill cancer cells in the body. It circulates your body in the bloodstream treating cancer cells almost anywhere in the body. It is known as systemic treatment and kills cells that are in the process of splitting into two new cells.

After Dave was done his treatment, he went for a PET (positron emission tomography) scan which is an imaging test that uses special dye with radioactive tracers. These tracers collect in areas where there is higher chemical activity such as cancer. These areas show up as bright spots on the

PET scan. The scan can find abnormal activity whereas a CT (computerized tomography) scan only shows detailed pictures of the organs and tissues inside your body. Dave will likely need continued PET scans to monitor and check for cancer recurrence.

As of now, Dave is in the clear. He needs to see his surgeon for a check-up every six months, as well as his oncologist every six months. He will need regular PET scans over the years but for now we are grateful to say he is in remission!

CHAPTER 28

TALKING ABOUT ALS

Amyotrophic Lateral Sclerosis (also known as ALS, Lou Gehrig's disease, or motor neuron disease) is a disease that gradually paralyzes people because the brain is no longer able to communicate with the muscles of the body that we are typically able to move at will. Over time, as the muscles of the body break down, someone living with ALS will lose the ability to walk, talk, eat, swallow, and eventually breathe.

After numerous tests to rule out anything else that could be wrong, my father-in-law was sent to the ALS clinic in Vancouver. After spending nearly five hours at the clinic, the ALS diagnosis was confirmed. The prognosis was 2-5 years but likely quicker due to my father-in-law's age and the type of ALS. His was called Bulbar ALS which starts in the respiratory system rather than the limbs. He would need a feeding tube, lots of rest, and around the clock care eventually.

My father-in-law's ALS journey was short but horrendous. In less than six months, he went from diagnosis to heaven bound. We watched him lose every ability he had. We watched him fight to the end until there was no fight left.

Through walking this ALS journey, I have learned how to have even more compassion. How can you not when you can see the life slowly being ripped away from your loved one. knowing there is absolutely nothing you can do about it. How can I not have compassion on Dave who was preparing to lose his dad before even knowing if he was going to survive cancer? How can I not have compassion on my family who has been through so much these past two years?

Through the ALS journey, I feel like our family has grown closer together, we have all learned a lot about this disorder as well as each other. We have learned how to be understanding of each other's needs while at the same time maintaining strong bonds between each other. The bonds between siblings are now tenfold compared to a year ago and I don't think anything will change that now. My father-in-law would be so proud to see his kids now.

CHAPTER 29

TALKING ABOUT FAITH

My faith journey started at the age of ten. No one told me about God before then. The next-door neighbours and their kids (my friend Kate with the engagement ring) went to a Friday night kids program and invited me to go along. Through them and their church I found God at ten years old. I didn't fully know or understand God at that point, and I knew I had a lot to learn. Now I am so thankful I took the time to know God and build that relationship because I have needed him so much through my life. There is no way I could get through half the things I have gone through without God beside me walking me through.

Throughout the years, my faith has brought me through some pretty difficult times. My first memory of putting all my trust in God was back in 2006. I was in high school, lived on my own in an apartment, and had a part time job. I used my spare block in school Monday to Friday to leave school early and start work until the mall closed at 5:30. I also had a Saturday shift I ultimately relied on that was my eight-hour shift. This was where I made the most of my money to go towards my rent, bills, and groceries. During one of my shifts, I was told the other worker needed his Saturday shift back to pay for schooling. This meant I was out $200 a month which I could not afford. I was still a high school student after all, I only had so much time. This was where it counted. This was where I needed to trust God with all my heart because He promises He will give us what we need.

A few days later, a family I used to babysit for asked me if I could start babysitting every Saturday for them for the next foreseeable future so they could have a date day together. They were offering me $50 a day. Well, being that there were four Saturdays in a month, that was exactly my missing $200 that I needed. Not only that but they asked if I would be willing to do some Sundays too which meant I could even get ahead! I trusted God and He came through for me.

In my relationship with Jesus, it is exactly that. I have a relationship with Him. I talk to Him through prayer, and He talks to me in various ways such as scripture, dreams, people, and situations. I remember one time He spoke to me in a dream. I had a dream that something had happened to my friend from church. I couldn't shake it for days; it was that real. That Sunday she was a greeter at church and as she greeted my hand, I told her I had a dream about her. Instantly, with a smile on her face, she asks if it was good. I told her no, it wasn't, but I didn't know what was wrong. I asked her if everything was okay in her life. She looked me in the eye, and said, "I just found out I have cancer." I couldn't believe it. God put her on my heart through a dream and I followed that instinct and prayed for her for days afterward. In hindsight I wish I had contacted her sooner, but I thought I might be crazy. I mean really, God talking to me in a dream. There isn't anything special about me. Oh, but there is. I was meant to have that dream and I was meant to pray for Wendy.

She let me walk alongside her for her journey even taking me along to some doctor's appointments, so she didn't have to drive alone. I was so happy to be able to walk alongside her during such a difficult time. Luckily, she is now cancer free and has been since 2015.

This situation like Wendy's has happened more and more. It's not that God tells me when bad things happen, but I do feel Him putting people on my heart to pray for them. I also feel called to reach out to these people. In my **Building Connections** ministry, when I feel called to pray for someone, I also reach out to message them. Often, there is something going on in this person's life (I mean, who doesn't have stuff going on in their life?). It helps for me to be able to step up and help by means of prayer, encouragement, or tangible help. Wendy's situation showed me just how important it is to go with my gut when I feel called to pray for someone or reach out to them. It never hurts to check on those around us.

When it comes to my relationship with Jesus, I need to be open and honest with Him as well as with myself, and He will guide me. In 1 Peter 5:7, the Bible says, "Cast all your cares and anxieties on him for he cares for you." This means when I am at my lowest of lows, I need Him. But I need to be open and honest in what is going on in my heart. For our friends, our family, our coworkers, we tell them the surface stuff. We tell them the top layer of what's really happening in our lives. God wants it all, He wants all the ugly. I'm not going to be free of all that's weighing me down unless I go to Him with all of it. He is there to walk with me through the valleys and over the mountaintops. But He wants all of me. After all, He is my creator.

CHAPTER 30
TALKING ABOUT WRITING A BOOK

So why did I put down 50,000 words and hours of my time writing this book? I'm glad you asked. Writing is so good for the brain when it comes to processing. It's hard for us to process our thoughts when they are circling so rampantly in our heads. Writing gives me the ability to grab hold of those wandering thoughts and put them into perspective. When I start writing, I almost never know what I am going to write. I believe some of the words are from my head, but I also believe some of the words are from God. I pray God would use my story to encourage others in whatever hardships come upon them.

I have gotten so much from writing my book. I started off just journaling our cancer story and before I knew it, I had a book. For me, writing has been therapeutic and essential for the processing and recovery of my mental health. I don't think anyone is meant to keep things bottled up inside. That can only last so long. For me, writing has allowed me to get all those feelings out; the facts, the feelings, the emotions, everything I was keeping bottled up.

I have friends I talk to, and I talk to Dave about almost everything but there was nothing quite like having my second child in the middle of a pandemic while my husband battled cancer. And then my father-in-law passed from ALS, I was diagnosed with PTSD, and Jesse was diagnosed with autism all by the end of the next calendar year. I feel like I could be in a better place mentally, but I also feel like I could be in a much worse place. I really do feel like writing has contributed to me staying somewhat sane throughout the last 24 months.

Throughout the last two years, I have seen God's provision, I saw His hand at work in my life and the lives of those around me. I saw people come together to form community. I saw with my own eyes, the building of bonds between family, community, and across the globe. I witnessed time and time again, God's story being written in the lives of those around me and I am so blessed to be a part of each and everyone's story. Thank you for taking the time to be a part of mine!

My family photo, October 2021

Manufactured by Amazon.ca
Bolton, ON

27595645R00111